Rise Biscuit

5 cups flour
2 TBS sugar
2 tsp baking powder
tsp salt
— soda

shortening.

—est in 1/4 cup

Corn Casserole

Serves:

Recipe from the kitchen of:
Marsha Lurey

2 (17 oz) cream style corn + 2 Tbs flour
1 c. milk
2 beaten eggs
1 c. coarsely ground saltines
1/4 c. fine chopped onion
3 Tbs. chopped pimento
3/4 tsp. salt
1/2 c. saltines
1 Tbs. butter

In And Out Potatoes
recipe from: Dolly Jones
serves: Your Good Friends

—rub Skins of Baking Potatoes.
Bake in Pre-heated oven… until A
—e a through them.
… a Sharp Knife
… Cacross

Here's what's cookin' Wheat Rolls
Recipe from the kitchen of
Serves

2 cups plain flour   1/4 cup sugar
2 pkgs. yeast   1 T. salt
1 cup milk   2 1/2 to 3 cup whole wheat flour
1/2 cup oil   3 1/4 c. water

—ift together flour and yeast. Heat milk,
water, oil, sugar and salt till very warm. Add
… to mixture. Beat at

Here's what's cookin' Sausage-Egg Casserole
Recipe from the kitchen of: Lyn Hunt   Serves: 4-5

6 lb. bulk sausage
6 slices white bread, crusts removed
softened butter (3 Tbs.)
Longhorn cheese
eggs
Half & Half   1 tsp. salt
1 tsp. dry mustard

Cook sausage —
Drain. Set aside
Spread bread w/

1/4 tsp. dried thyme leaves
1/4 tsp. pepper
1/4 c. + 2 Tbs. olive oil

Heat oven to 400°
Place tomatoes in

German Ch—

1 c. sugar   1 frozen pie she—
1 Tbs. cornstarch   2 Tbs. Fl—
2 eggs   pinch of salt
2/3 c. milk   3 Tbs. melted butte—
3/4 c. shredded coconut
1/2 c. chopped pecans   1 tsp. vanilla

Mix together. Put in blender ab—
Blend until smo…

Creole Shrimp

1 C chopped onion
1/2 c. green pepper
1-2 ribs of celery
1 small garlic clove crushed
2 Tbl bacon drippings
3 Tbl. flour
1 (16 oz) can peeled tomatoes
1 (3 oz) tomato paste
1 tsp fresh green parsley

1/4 tsp Cayenne pepper
1/2 tsp gr. mace
1/8 tsp sugar
1/2 tsp lemon pepper marinade
1 tbl Worcestershire
1/8 tsp paprika
1 beef bouillon (and 1 c. boiling water)

My Pet Recipe for Swedish Meat Balls

3 # gr beef

Here's what's cookin' Pecan Dump Cake   Serves
Recipe from the kitchen of   Debbie Tamplin

Grease + flour 9 x 13" pan.
Empty (1 lb.) can crushed pineapple into pan and spread
evenly. Sprinkle 1 c. light brown
sugar over pineapple. Spread
1 pkg. yellow cake mix (dry) over the
brown sugar. Put 1 c. chopped nuts on top
of cake mix, 2 sticks melted butter on top
of nuts. Bake at 325° about 50 min.

pkg. hash browns
melted butter
salt + pepper
sour cream
chopped onion
cream of chicken so—
cup cheddar cheese
Pan- layer ha—

Recipe from the kitchen of
S. C. A. STEWART, JR.

1/2 c. brown sugar
1/4 c. Catsup
3/4 c. water
Salt and pepper chops.
shallow pan. Combine
sugar, catsup and wat—
over chops. Bake at 350° f—

Lord,
How did I do it?

V5

baking powder
c. milk
Potato
JARVIS

The VERYVERA COOKBOOK

recipes from my table

Enjoy these recipes
on Your table!

Vera

The VERYVERA COOKBOOK

recipes from my table

VERA STEWART

PHOTOGRAPHY BY PETER FRANK EDWARDS

STORY FARM

WINTER PARK * MIAMI * SANTA BARBARA

PUBLISHED IN THE UNITED STATES BY STORY FARM, LLC.

WWW.STORY-FARM.COM

LIBRARY OF CONGRESS CATALOGING-IN-PUBLICATION DATA

AVAILABLE UPON REQUEST

ISBN-13: 978-0-9969441-6-8

EDITORIAL DIRECTOR ASHLEY FRAXEDAS

ART DIRECTOR LAUREN EGGERT

PROJECT MANAGER RACHEL SCHIFTER

CREATIVE MANAGER EMILY YATES

COPY EDITORS KAREN CAKEBREAD, CASSANDRA PALMER

STYLIST SANDY LANG

INDEXING AMY HALL

PRODUCTION MANAGER TINA DAHL

10 9 8 7 6 5 4

FOURTH EDITION

PRINTED IN CHINA

BETTY STEWART WINGFIELD
1917-1984

To Mama
One of the strongest women I've
ever known and my first mentor.

Table
OF CONTENTS

it all starts with a recipe

I've always had a fascination with recipes. I remember the excitement of seeing my mother pull the recipe box down from the top of the refrigerator, knowing that we were getting ready to make something delicious. My grandmother thought my handwriting was pretty, so she would ask me to rewrite some of her favorites.

I used to pick out packets of recipe cards with vintage illustrations to give as gifts, and I loved collecting cherished recipes from family and friends. I never dreamed at that time that this interest would turn into a career and, ultimately, a book full of my own recipes—the one that you're now holding.

My journey with VeryVera actually started early. The events of my childhood fostered my "get the job done" attitude. When you're the middle of five children, as I was, it's easy to get overlooked, so I learned early how to get attention, which would come to serve me well later in my career. My dad died at the age of

FROM LEFT: MY GRANDMOTHER VERA AND MAMA, BETTY; ALL MY SIBLINGS ON EASTER SUNDAY, CIRCA 1960; MY FIRST MENTOR, MAMA BETTY; CATHERINE DUPREE, MY SECOND MENTOR.

forty, leaving my mother to raise all five of us by herself. My life from that point on was guided by a strong female influence. My mother expected the best from each of us in order to keep the ship sailing smoothly. Looking back, she was my first mentor. She was an educator, and like other key educators I had in school, she instilled in me organizational skills, psychological insights, a strong-willed personality, and personal pride. My second mentor would be my senior-year homeroom teacher, Catherine Dupree. A single mom herself, she was a passionate home economics instructor whose class spoke directly to my first love—cooking. Her encouragement led me to the University of Georgia to major in home economics education, putting me on the career path that I have followed to this day.

COTTAGE INDUSTRY

I began teaching home economics in Marietta, Georgia, in 1974 at the age of twenty-one. I got married the following summer and moved to Madison, Georgia, where I took over a recently vacated teaching position at Morgan County High School. In 1978, we moved to Cartersville, Georgia, where there were no open teaching positions, which turned out to be a blessing in disguise. I spent that year hosting new friends and showcasing my love for both entertaining

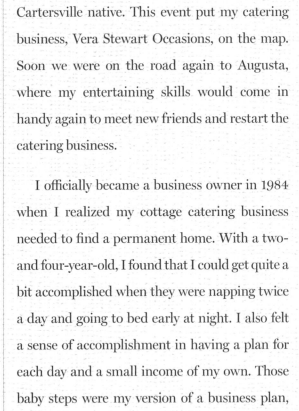

and food preparation. Our son John was born in 1979, and then Daniel in 1982. During that time, I was fortunate enough to cater small dinner parties and receptions in the Cartersville area. I managed to land the inaugural luncheon for the staff of Governor Joe Frank Harris, a Cartersville native. This event put my catering business, Vera Stewart Occasions, on the map. Soon we were on the road again to Augusta, where my entertaining skills would come in handy again to meet new friends and restart the catering business.

I officially became a business owner in 1984 when I realized my cottage catering business needed to find a permanent home. With a two- and four-year-old, I found that I could get quite a bit accomplished when they were napping twice a day and going to bed early at night. I also felt a sense of accomplishment in having a plan for each day and a small income of my own. Those baby steps were my version of a business plan, and I've evolved that strategy over thirty-plus years. During this time I was fortunate enough to be introduced as one of the leading caterers in Augusta, and since Augusta hosts a very large golf tournament in April each year, my name was mentioned in some very large circles. I went from doing sweet-sixteen teas to hosting elaborate dinners for corporations and working alongside some of the most notable event planners in the country. We are fortunate to have many of those clients still part of our family today. I learned much from these experienced professionals that I was able to share with my local clients.

In 1986, I happened upon an advertisement in *Country Living* for a cooking seminar with rising culinary star Martha Stewart. My husband agreed to watch the boys while I took a trip to Westport, Connecticut, to learn under a woman who would change the face of catering. Thus, I met the third mentor of my life. Her influence early in my career steered me in the right direction with the proper sense of purpose.

MAIL ORDER

The next ten years kept me extremely busy, but the overhead cost of operating from a commercial location made it impossible to have

a steady income. VeryVera began to diversify out of necessity. My desire to create a constant income led to an experiment in the summer of 1993. I put my grandmother's pound cake in a tin and shipped it to friends and family all over the country with only a few questions for feedback: "How did this pound cake look when you opened the tin? Was it in one piece? How did it taste?" The remarks were favorable, and so I launched VeryVera, the mail-order division of Vera Stewart Occasions. I named my business "VeryVera" after my 4-foot-11-inch grandmother,

FROM LEFT: DANIEL (2) AND JOHN (4); VERA STUDYING UNDER MARTHA STEWART IN 1986.

Vera Wright Wingfield, who won the nickname because everything she did was just "very Vera." In 1996, we launched *veryvera.com* and were years ahead of most other companies presenting similar products. We increased our product line from pound cakes to layer cakes and perfected a packaging with a 95 percent success rate. They arrived looking so pretty, in fact, that most of the cakes that appeared in magazine or newspaper articles through the years were photographed right out of the box that arrived by UPS or FedEx.

In 2001, we added the beloved casseroles, salads, and sides enjoyed by catering clients to our mail-order line, and we called this addition Gourmet to Go. We then saw the need to expand to include a café where customers could come in to eat. The VeryVera Café became a favorite in Augusta and to all that passed Exit 199 on I-20. These additions and changes opened up more jobs and possibilities for expansion, so we sought out other online mail-order companies to consider our products. Saks, Neiman Marcus, Costco, Bloomingdale's, Horchow, and HSN all jumped on board with us, and off we went! The year 2004 brought more diversification when I created a summer cooking camp for children and brought my career full circle, as I became a home economics teacher again.

THROWDOWN TO TV

When the call came in 2010 from the brand-new Cooking Channel® to ask if I would consider myself an expert on carrot cake, my answer was certainly "yes." I had no way of knowing I would be in a battle with Bobby Flay on a Food Network® "Throwdown"—and beat him. This

FROM LEFT: THE VERYVERA CAFE; THE VERYVERA COOKBOOK COVER; TYLER FLORENCE AS A GUEST DURING SEASON 1 OF THE VERYVERA SHOW.

experience opened other TV doors, and WAGT in Augusta offered me my own cooking show. Season 1 of *The VeryVera Show* aired in 2012. Since then, the show has won a couple of Merit GABBY awards and has been syndicated into various other markets. The vintage recipe cards that appear in each episode's opening segment are the same that started me on this journey as a child.

JUDGE A BOOK BY ITS COVER

When I closed my retail operation in July 2013, it was my goal to work hard on syndicating *The VeryVera Show*, franchising VeryVera Cooking Camp, and writing *The VeryVera Cookbook*. You are now holding the realization of my final goal, and it has made me enormously proud. You may not have noticed, but there's some significance to the gorgeous cover of this book.

I've always loved old things. Growing up without my dad, I appreciated that my mother and my grandmother were college educated. They grew up in an environment where things like pretty silver, a well-set table, and traditional celebrations had great meaning. The picture of my grandmother with her sorority sisters on the cover of this book was a pretty picture to me as a child, and my mother loved to point out the similarities in our physical features. Later, as a Phi Mu at the University of Georgia, those ties to other young women meant the most to me in

my college experience. Most people thought the picture of my mother as a girl was a picture of me dressed up in vintage clothes. My mother would have been 100 on the day we shot this cover. The now-classic photo of Vera and Betty (my grandmother and mother) was my sister Bitsy's find years ago when I asked all of my siblings for any picture they might have of my grandmother. As VeryVera was my grandmother's namesake, I needed a great picture of Vera to use in marketing. I was thrilled when this picture emerged, so it became the face of the company.

The components of the table represent old and new, my style of presentation, and a composite of vessels that make the table unique. As a student of Martha Stewart, I learned that merging components and varying materials make a statement for any event. The flowers display my classic "just see what's in your yard or your neighbor's yard" technique, and the container has been used a million times over the course of my career in events. The silver knives were buried in the creek when Sherman marched through Georgia, and the caramel cake was present at every family reunion I attended until my Aunt Libba Mullins died. The potato salad had to go on the table last because it's best served warm, and someone could be walking up with a loaf of white bread for the pimento cheese. The horseshoe may be my favorite part, as I know you think it's for good luck. For me, it's a reminder that you can't wait for luck. Hard work is the only way to make your dreams come true. I was honored to work with the renowned photographer Peter Frank Edwards for this project. I was blown away by his willingness to indulge my whims to make sure each photo told the story of VeryVera.

FROM LEFT: VERA RECREATING THE CLASSIC "VERA AND BETTY" PHOTO; A COLLECTION OF VERA'S RECIPE CARDS.

Rise Biscuit

5 cups flour
2 TBS sugar
2 tsp baking powder
~~ tsp salt
~~ soda

—hortening.

...est in 1/4 cup

Corn Casserole

Recipe from the kitchen of:

Marsha Lurey

Serves:

2 (17 oz) cream style corn   + 2 Tbs flour
1 c. milk
2 beaten eggs
1 c. coarsely ground saltines
1/4 c. fine chopped onion
3 Tbs. chopped pimento
3/4 tsp. salt
pepper
1/2 c. saltines
1 Tbs. butter

Cookin' Hot Herbed

Recipe from: Katie Flanagan
2 (16) cans Hunt's whole to
3/4 c. soft bread crumbs
1/4 c. plus 2 Tbs. minced on
1/4 c. + 2 Tbs. parsley (put on
1 lg. clove garlic, minced
3/4 tsp. salt
1/3 tsp. dried thyme leaves
1/4 tsp. pepper
1/4 c. + 2 Tbs. olive oil

Heat oven to 4000
Place tomatoes in

here's who...

In And Out Potatoes
recipe from: Dolly Jones
serves: Your Good Friends

~~rub Skins of Baking Potatoes.
~~ake in Pre-heated oven....Until A
~~ce through them.
~~h a Sharp Knife
~~ (across

Here's what's cookin' **Wheat Rolls**
Recipe from the kitchen of   Serves

2 cups plain flour   1/4 cup sugar
2 pkgs. yeast   1 T. salt
1 cup milk   2 1/2 to 3 cup whole wheat flour
1/2 cup oil   3 1/4 c water

Sift together flour and yeast. Heat milk
water, oil, sugar, and salt till very warm. Add
~~ mixture. Beat at

Here's what's cookin: **Sausage-Egg Casserole**
Recipe from the kitchen of: Lyn Hunt   Serves: 4-5
1 lb. bulk sausage
6 slices white bread   crusts removed
softened butter
(3 Tbs)
Longhorn cheese
eggs
Half & Half   1 tsp. salt
1 tsp. dry mustard

Cook sausage —
Drain. Set aside
Spread bread w/

KITCHEN OF: Mary Fran
Squash Casserole

~~elted butter
~~ squash, thinly s

~~apple
~~mellow~~naise
~~ green pepper
~~ onion

German Ch

1 c. sugar
1 Tbs. cornstarch   2 Tbs
pinch of salt
2 eggs   3 Tbs. melted butter
2/3 c. milk   1 tsp. vanilla
3/4 c. shredded coconut
Blend until sm~~   chopped pecans

1 frozen pie she~~

Here's
Recipe
Place 2/3

Creole Shrimp

1 C chopped onion
1/2 c
~~ green pepper
1-2 ribs of celery
1 small garlic clove crushed
2 Tbl bacon drippings
3 Tbl. flour
1 (16 oz) can peeled tomatoes
1 (3 oz) tomato paste
~~ dried green parsley

1/4 tsp. cayenne pepper
1/2 tsp. gr. mace
1/8 tsp. sugar
2 tsp lemon pepper
marinade
1 Tbl Worcestershire
1/8 tsp paprika

My PET RECIPE for

Swedish Meat Balls

3 # gr beef
1 ~~ sausage~~
~~ mix well & make~~

...S. C. A. STEWART, JR.

...n the kitchen of

Claire Cook

Here's what's cookin' **Pecan Dump Cake** Serves
Recipe from the kitchen of   Debbie Tamplin

Grease & flour 9"×13" pan.
Empty (1 lb.) can crushed pineapple into pan and spread
evenly. Sprinkle 1 c. light brown
sugar over pineapple. Spread
1 pkg. yellow cake mix (dry) over the
brown sugar. Put 1 c. chopped nuts on top
of cake mix, 2 sticks melted butter on top
of nuts. Bake at 325° about 50 min.

---

pkg. hash browns
melted butter
salt + pepper
sour cream
chopped onion
cream of chicken
~~p cheddar cheese
Pan- layer ha~~
ingredi~~
~~Pork Chops

Heat oven to 3
qt casserole. Cook
divided,
baking,
eggs & a

Aspic

~~ Pepper
~~Pork Chops
~~ c brown sugar
1/4 c Catsup
3/4 c water
Salt and pepper chops
shallow pan. Combine
sugar, Catsup and water
over chops. Bake at 350°
Cover for first hour a~~
Turn Chops at least one~~

~~ loaves wh~~
one side light

Add 1 pkg. herb se~~

Cook onion, celery
(all diced)

Potato
~~da Jarvis
~~tsp. baking

A DREAM FULFILLED

Years ago, I catered the grand opening for a paper company's newest facility, and the original founder's grandson, now the company's CEO, stood to welcome the attendees. He said in his remarks, "I am so proud of the company that my grandfather founded." Holding back tears, I looked at my catering team members and said, "That's what I want! I want one of my grandchildren to say that one day." In closing VeryVera's retail operation, most of my emotion stemmed from the fact that this opportunity seemed to be fading. I've realized that through *The VeryVera Show*, VeryVera Cooking Camp, and now this very special book, the VeryVera Enterprises brand has stayed alive and thrived. Who knows, maybe this book will keep things going until one of my grandchildren decides they want to take over Granny V's business.

Writing this book has been an extremely nostalgic experience. I have mentally revisited

FROM LEFT: THE FRONT WALL OF THE VERYVERA COTTAGE; VERA AND PHOTOGRAPHER PETER FRANK EDWARDS AT VERA'S BEAUFORT HOME DURING A COOKBOOK PHOTO SHOOT.

every day in the bakery as I personally tested each cake, sweet treat, and savory recipe until they were exactly as I remembered. I have relived waiting tables in the Café and having customers order the "PCC" (Pecan Crusted Chicken Salad, page 58) or The Grill (page 28). I had so much fun with the little green ticket book in my hand and my black-and-white checkered smock. I have remembered that I sent Oprah cakes for ten years before she wrote about our Strawberry Layer Cake (page 107) and that when *Southern Living* trusted our cakes enough in 1996 to write a two-thirds-page editorial about them, we made a sale in every state in less than ten days. I have recalled the nights I called my husband to say I wouldn't be coming home because we were going to bake through the night. I have remembered the urgent calls to the Styrofoam® cooler company when the temperature went into the upper 90s around Mother's Day and we had to put every cake in a cooler with dry ice. I laugh now, but I cried when the ice storm hit, causing us to lose everything in our kitchen two days before Valentine's Day orders shipped.

Proceed into this book with the intent to remember one of the favorites you used to order online, send to a friend, eat in our Café, enjoy at an event, or read about in a magazine. I know there are those that spent close to twenty years ordering the same cake on your birthday or for someone special. I hope you will try your hand at making it yourself. Don't be intimidated by anything. Believe me when I say I tested them all and know they taste just like what you ordered from us. Who knows, they might even taste better when you make them yourself!

ABOVE, FROM LEFT: O, THE OPRAH MAGAZINE, PAULA DEEN MAGAZINE, SAKS 5TH AVENUE CATALOG, AND THE SOUTHERN LIVING ARTICLE THAT PUT VERYVERA ON THE MAP. OPPOSITE PAGE, CLOCKWISE, FROM TOP: MCCLENDON (2), LUCY (4), JANE (6), FRANCES (18 MONTHS), AND WARD (8 MONTHS); PINCKNEY (16); MADISON (15); MCCORD (12); BENTLEY (13).

If you're new to VeryVera, welcome to the family. You will learn more about the company as you read through this book because every recipe tells a story. I hope this will become one of your favorite cookbooks as you experience why our products were so popular.

My wish is that this book will inspire you to make memories in the kitchen, be generous with your culinary creations, and chase your dreams, just as I have chased mine.

Vera

breads, spreads
& OTHER SOUTHERN BITES

*d*on't ever underestimate the first bite of a meal. The breads, spreads, and other Southern bites are a crucial accompaniment to any successful gathering. The recipes in this chapter will help you start the meal off right! Here are a few notes before we get started.

RECIPES

When it comes to recipes, always follow the instructions exactly. This includes following the suggestion for using brand-name ingredients. If brands are noted in the recipe, please use my suggestion. If a brand is not noted, don't skimp on the quality of the ingredient. A finished product will only be as good as the ingredients used to prepare it.

Unlike the spreads and breads that you purchase at the grocery store, VeryVera's versions have never contained preservatives. Therefore, please note the 6-day shelf life on most of our recipes. These foods should always be stored in an airtight container or a resealable plastic bag. Allowing extra air into the product will quicken the staling process.

FREEZING BREADS

If making bread to freeze for use later, reduce the baking time by a few minutes, to prevent overdoneness in reheating. To freeze bread, I suggest wrapping it tightly in plastic wrap and then placing it in an airtight container. This will help avoid freezer burn. Bread can be frozen for up to 6 months. Let the bread defrost completely before reheating. One trick to reheat bread without drying it out is to microwave it under a damp paper towel for 5- to 10-second intervals until it is warmed through.

GIFTS

Food always makes a great gift. This can be a hostess gift, a gift to welcome a new baby, a housewarming gift, or a gift to send to your favorite college student. Unique packaging can transform a recipe drop-off to something you see featured in a magazine. Invited to dinner? I suggest taking the Vidalia Onion Dip (page 32) to start the party off with a bang. Enjoy!

choosing your ingredients

SPICES

The spices used in these recipes are very important, as this is where you control most of the flavor. When storing dry spices, be sure to keep them in a dark and cool place in your kitchen. This will help maintain the potency of the spices for a longer time. Spices typically have very long expiration dates, but check them occasionally to ensure you're not using expired ingredients in your recipes.

VIDALIA ONIONS

Vidalia onions are Georgia-grown, naturally sweet, and add an extra richness to any recipe calling for onions. This is the type of onion that I prefer to use in most of the recipes throughout this book. Although it's possible to find Vidalia onions outside Georgia, it can be difficult. If these onions are not available in your area, try another sweet onion, but I do not recommend a strong onion when a Vidalia onion is suggested.

pimento cheese

Pimento cheese has a multitude of variations, and in the South, people fight over whose is the best. At VeryVera, we had customers that came in just for the pimento cheese. Unlike traditional pimento cheese recipes that call for jarred pimentos, mine uses roasted red peppers, which add a welcome smoky element.

SERVES: 6 TO 8 (MAKES APPROXIMATELY 4 CUPS) | PREP TIME: 15 MINUTES

1 CUP ROASTED RED PEPPERS

1¼ POUNDS CRACKER BARREL® SHARP CHEDDAR CHEESE, HAND-SHREDDED

¼ TEASPOON CAYENNE PEPPER

¼ TEASPOON COARSE BLACK PEPPER, OR MORE TO TASTE

½ TEASPOON TONY CHACHERE® CREOLE SEASONING

2 CUPS DUKE'S® MAYONNAISE

1. Slice the red peppers into ¼-inch strips. Cut the strips on the bias to make small chunks.

2. Pat the red pepper pieces dry.

3. Combine all the ingredients. Do not overmix.

4. Store in an airtight container in the refrigerator for up to 3 weeks.

SERVING SUGGESTION:

THE GRILL SANDWICH: HOMEMADE PIMENTO CHEESE ON MARBLED RYE WITH 3 STRIPS OF COOKED BACON AND TOMATO SLICES, LIGHTLY GRILLED.

THE GIFT IS IN THE MAIL

When the food columnist for the New York Times, *Marian Burros, chooses your product for the special "The Gift Is in the Mail" issue that runs in early November for the holidays, you might as well put an Oscar next to this item on the shelf! We were very proud of this 2007 accolade.*

A book called American Sandwich *by Becky Mercuri, published in 2004, selected VeryVera's pimento cheese as the state sandwich for Georgia. I gave them the recipe for our café's "The Grill Sandwich," but they had to find another recipe for pimento cheese—I haven't published mine until now!*

THE NY TIMES, NOVEMBER 2007

FEATURED IN

NY Times *The Gift Is in the Mail*

CHEDDAR CHEESE AND CHIVE BISCUITS

Like any biscuit, I love these with breakfast, lunch, or dinner. This recipe takes the classic butter-milk biscuit and spins it in a different direction with a bite of sharp cheddar cheese and green onion. Enjoy these with butter or create a biscuit sandwich! One of the most popular breads in our Gourmet to Go line, these biscuits dress up dinner with their first impression and then the first bite brings the WOW!

MAKES: 24 BISCUITS | PREP TIME: 25 MINUTES | BAKE TIME: 7 TO 8 MINUTES

½ cup lard, cut into small cubes and chilled

4 cups self-rising flour

1 cup sharp cheddar cheese, hand-shredded

½ cup green onions, chopped

1½ cups buttermilk, chilled

Self-rising flour, for dusting

2 tablespoons salted butter, melted

1. Preheat the oven to 500°F and line a rimmed baking sheet with parchment paper.

2. In a large bowl, cut the lard into the flour with a pastry blender or two forks until the mixture is crumbly. The crumbles should be pea-sized and the flour should start to look like wet sand.

3. Add the cheddar cheese and green onions, stirring just until the ingredients are coated with flour. Add the buttermilk and stir just until the dry ingredients are moistened.

4. Turn the dough out onto a floured work surface and sprinkle with the self-rising flour.

5. Knead the dough 2 to 3 times or until it is smooth.

6. Pat the dough into a ¾-inch-thick rectangle.

7. Cut out biscuits with a floured 2-inch round cutter, being careful not to twist the cutter. Twisting the cutter can seal the edges of the biscuit, which could prevent the biscuits from rising. Reshape the scraps as needed to finish cutting.

8. Place the biscuits with sides touching on the prepared baking sheet.

9. Bake for 7 to 8 minutes or until golden brown. Remove from the oven and brush the tops of the baked biscuits with melted salted butter.

10. Let cool completely on the baking sheet. Serve warm or store in an airtight container.

NOTE: THESE BISCUITS FREEZE BEAUTIFULLY. WRAP THE FROZEN BISCUITS IN FOIL AND PLACE IN A 350°F OVEN FOR 20 MINUTES TO HEAT.

vidalia onion dip

This dip is Southern to its core and completely irresistible. If you can find them, Vidalia onions from Vidalia, Georgia, are my first choice for this recipe. If you're unable to get your hands on Vidalias, regular sweet onions will work. I serve this dip with Fritos Scoops!® corn chips, but you can choose any chip or cracker you prefer.

MAKES: APPROXIMATELY 5 TO 6 CUPS | PREP TIME: 20 MINUTES | COOK TIME: 15 TO 20 MINUTES

16 OUNCES CREAM CHEESE, AT ROOM TEMPERATURE

1⅓ CUPS PARMESAN CHEESE, HAND-SHREDDED

⅓ CUP HELLMANN'S® MAYONNAISE

3 CUPS VIDALIA ONIONS, DICED

1. Preheat the oven to 325°F and prepare a 9-inch pie dish with cooking spray.

2. Combine the cream cheese, Parmesan cheese, and mayonnaise with a mixer on medium speed, or until just blended.

3. Stir in the onions by hand.

4. Scoop into the prepared 9-inch pie dish.

5. Bake for 15 to 20 minutes, or until bubbly and browned on the top.

6. Serve hot.

OTHER USES:

- ADD DIP TO TWICE-BAKED POTATOES TO MAKE THEM EXTRA CREAMY AND FLAVORFUL.

- STUFF DIP INSIDE A HAMBURGER TO MAKE THE ULTIMATE CROWD-PLEASER.

- FILL SMALL PHYLLO CUPS WITH THE UNCOOKED DIP AND RUN THEM UNDER THE BROILER UNTIL LIGHTLY BROWNED FOR A QUICK, PASSED APPETIZER. SERVE WITH TOMATO RELISH AND BACON.

NOTE: IN THE MAIL-ORDER BUSINESS, THE GOAL IS TO INTRODUCE AS MANY PEOPLE AS POSSIBLE TO YOUR PRODUCTS. WHEN MARIAN BURROS OF THE *NEW YORK TIMES* RECOGNIZED OUR VIDALIA ONION DIP IN THE 2007 "THE GIFT IS IN THE MAIL" FEATURE ARTICLE, WE HAD FANS FROM COAST TO COAST!

CHEESE STRAWS

A true Southern snack, cheese straws are found in many shapes and textures. These are crisp, cheesy, and toasty with a little heat thanks to cayenne pepper. They make for the ultimate Southern hostess gift. They are even a favorite of Georgia Senator Johnny Isakson. We made them in a pasta machine at VeryVera, but I recommend an electric cookie press. We do not recommend freezing these, as their texture doesn't hold up through freezing and defrosting. These are best enjoyed fresh, but do have a 1-month shelf life if stored in an airtight container.

MAKES: 10 DOZEN STRAWS | PREP TIME: 45 MINUTES | COOK TIME: 10 TO 12 MINUTES

1 pound (4 cups) Cracker Barrel® sharp cheddar cheese

½ cup unsalted butter, at room temperature

½ cup shortening, at room temperature

2½ cups all-purpose flour

1 teaspoon salt

1 teaspoon dry mustard

¼ teaspoon cayenne pepper

1. Preheat the oven to 350°F.

2. Grate the cheese using a rotary grater or the finest setting on a box grater.

3. With a mixer on medium to high speed, cream the butter and shortening until soft.

4. Add the cheese and mix well.

5. Sift the flour, salt, mustard, and cayenne pepper together in a separate bowl. Add to the cheese mixture in three additions, mixing well after each addition.

6. Fill a cookie press with the cheese dough.

7. Using the saw-toothed disk, dispense onto a cookie sheet. Each cheese straw should be about 1 inch in length.

8. Bake for 10 to 12 minutes, or until the cheese straws are just starting to turn golden brown at the edges.

9. Carefully transfer the cheese straws to a wire rack for cooling.

10. Store in an airtight container for up to 1 month.

HALF & HALF

OUR BITE-SIZED TREATS, CHEESE STRAWS AND PECAN SANDIES (PAGE 139), WERE ALWAYS SO POPULAR THAT WE EVENTUALLY PUT THEM TOGETHER IN ONE TIN AS THE PERFECT FOOD GIFT. LOCAL AND MAIL-ORDER CUSTOMERS ALIKE ABSOLUTELY LOVED THE COMBINATION OF SALTY AND SWEET THAT WE SOLD UNDER THE NAME "HALF & HALF."

buttermilk biscuits

These biscuits were a staple for our family because buttermilk was always in our refrigerator. They melt in your mouth straight out of the oven. Serve and enjoy with butter, honey, your favorite jams and jellies, or either of my fantastic spreads—Bacon and Tomato Spread (page 39) or Honey Pecan Spread (page 39). Make these with an 8-year-old if you want to see the magic of baking come to life!

MAKES: 18 BISCUITS | PREP TIME: 20 MINUTES | BAKE TIME: 13 TO 15 MINUTES

3½ CUPS SELF-RISING FLOUR

2 TEASPOONS BAKING POWDER

2 TEASPOONS GRANULATED SUGAR

¼ CUP SHORTENING, CUT INTO SMALL CUBES AND CHILLED

¼ CUP UNSALTED BUTTER, CUT INTO SMALL CUBES AND CHILLED

1½ CUPS BUTTERMILK, CHILLED

SELF-RISING FLOUR, FOR DUSTING

2 TABLESPOONS SALTED BUTTER, MELTED

1. Preheat the oven to 450°F and line a rimmed baking sheet with parchment paper.

2. In a large bowl, whisk together the flour, baking powder, and sugar.

3. Scatter the chilled shortening and butter over the flour mixture, and toss lightly to coat the shortening and butter.

4. Cut in the shortening and butter with a pastry blender or two forks until the mixture is crumbly. The crumbles should be pea-sized and the flour should start to look like wet sand.

5. Add the buttermilk, stirring just until the dry ingredients are moistened.

6. Turn the dough out onto a floured work surface and sprinkle with the self-rising flour.

7. Knead the dough 4 to 5 times or until it is smooth and springy to the touch. Keep dusting with self-rising flour as needed to keep the dough from sticking to the work surface.

8. Pat the dough down to a ¾-inch thickness.

9. Cut out the biscuits with a floured 2-inch round cutter, being careful not to twist the cutter. Twisting the cutter can seal the edges of the biscuit, which could prevent the biscuits from rising. Reshape the scraps as needed to finish cutting.

10. Place the biscuits with sides touching on the prepared baking sheet.

11. Bake for 13 to 15 minutes or until golden brown. Remove from the oven and brush the tops of the baked biscuits with melted salted butter.

12. Let cool completely on the baking sheet. Serve warm or store in an airtight container.

HONEY PECAN SPREAD

What's better than a buttermilk biscuit? A buttermilk biscuit with Honey Pecan Spread. This simple spread is so easy to make, and it's the perfect accompaniment to serve with my Buttermilk Biscuits (page 36). I love to drizzle a little local honey on top at serving time. It's delicious, it makes for a beautiful presentation, and the local honey will help with allergies.

MAKES: APPROXIMATELY 1 CUP | PREP TIME: 5 TO 10 MINUTES

5⅓ ounces cream cheese, at room temperature

2 tablespoons local honey, plus more for garnish

2 tablespoons pecan halves, chopped

1. With a mixer, beat the cream cheese and honey.

2. Fold in the pecan pieces by hand.

3. Drizzle with honey before serving.

4. Store in an airtight container in the refrigerator for up to 6 days.

SERVING SUGGESTIONS:

1. Toast round + honey pecan spread + tomato jam or relish

2. Toasted cocktail-size biscuit + honey pecan spread + fig preserves + goat cheese + crispy bacon bite

BACON AND TOMATO SPREAD

My mother-in-law, Sue Stewart, used to say, "If you don't have time to start dinner before your husband gets home, throw some bacon in a pan to start frying. That way, he at least thinks something yummy is happening in the kitchen!" This spread takes everything you love about bacon and puts it into an easy and versatile spread that's great as a cocktail sandwich.

MAKES: APPROXIMATELY 2 CUPS | PREP TIME: 15 MINUTES

6 slices center-cut bacon

8 ounces cream cheese, at room temperature

2 tablespoons Hellmann's® mayonnaise

¾ teaspoon garlic powder

1 cup Roma tomatoes, chopped

1 tablespoon green onions, diced

1. Cook the bacon and when cool enough to handle, crumble and set aside.

2. Stir the softened cream cheese and mayonnaise until smooth.

3. Add the garlic powder and the crumbled bacon to the cream cheese mixture and mix well.

4. Scrape the sides of the bowl.

5. Fold in the tomatoes and green onions by hand. Do not overmix after adding the tomatoes, as they will get mushy.

6. Store in an airtight container in the refrigerator for up to 6 days.

YEAST ROLLS

These classic Southern rolls were a signature item at any wedding I catered in my 30-plus-year career. Jack Markwalter said it best when he hired me for his daughter's wedding: "The beef tenderloin better be medium-rare and those rolls better melt in my mouth." So many people are intimidated by yeast rolls and never try to make them because they seem complicated. Don't be one of those people! This recipe is simple, and the end result truly does melt in your mouth. They're a delicious bread option for a meal and also make a great base for a mini sandwich. Consider your use to determine the size of cutter to use.

MAKES: 50 ROLLS | PREP TIME: 2½ HOURS | BAKE TIME: 10 TO 12 MINUTES

2 (¼-ounce) envelopes active dry yeast

1¼ cups warm water (100°F to 112°F), divided

4½ to 5 cups all-purpose flour, divided

3 large eggs, lightly beaten

½ cup shortening, melted

½ cup granulated sugar

2 teaspoons salt

2 sticks unsalted butter, chilled and cut into 50 small pieces

1. Stir together the yeast and ¼ cup of the warm water in a liquid measuring cup and let stand for 5 minutes.

2. In the mixing bowl of a stand mixer, blend together the yeast mixture, the remaining 1 cup of warm water, 2 cups of the flour, the eggs, shortening, sugar, and salt.

3. Beat the mixture for at least 2 minutes or until a dough starts to form.

4. Gradually add the remaining flour, just enough to make a soft dough, and beat until just combined.

5. Cover the bowl and let the dough rise in a warm place (80°F to 85°F) for 1 hour.

6. Punch down the dough, cover, and chill in the refrigerator for at least 8 hours or overnight.

7. After the dough has chilled, punch down the dough again.

8. Turn the dough out onto a floured surface and knead about 4 times. Do not over-knead the dough.

9. Roll the dough to ½-inch thickness and brush off any excess flour.

10. Cut out the dough using a floured 2-inch biscuit cutter.

11. Place a small pat of butter in the center of the cut roll and fold in half with the butter on the inside.

12. Place on a greased or parchment-lined sheet pan and make sure the rolls are touching.

13. Cover the pan and let the rolls rise in a warm place for 1½ hours or until doubled in size.

14. While the rolls are rising, preheat the oven to 375°F.

15. Bake for 10 to 12 minutes or until golden brown.

16. Let cool on the pan. Serve warm or let the rolls cool completely before storing in an airtight container.

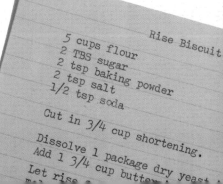

SOUR CREAM MUFFINS

"Could we have some more sour cream muffins?" was the most common request in our café. The bread basket offered all of our breads, but these were the clear favorite. These three-ingredient muffins may not sound like much, but they're so moist and versatile. I prefer to make mine in a mini muffin tin for pop-in-your-mouth muffins. This is a great recipe to make with grandchildren!

MAKES: 24 MINI MUFFINS | PREP TIME: 10 MINUTES | BAKE TIME: 20 MINUTES

Floured baking spray

2 cups self-rising flour

½ cup unsalted butter, melted

1 cup sour cream

1. Preheat the oven to 325°F.

2. Prepare a 24-cup mini muffin pan with floured baking spray.

3. In a large bowl, combine all the ingredients and mix until just combined. Be careful not to overmix the batter.

4. Spoon the batter into the prepared muffin pan. The batter should fill to the top of each mold.

5. Bake for 20 minutes or until lightly golden brown.

6. Let cool slightly in the pan before removing the muffins. Serve warm or let cool completely before storing.

SWEET POTATO ROLLS

The Sweet Potato Roll is a delightful twist to everyone's favorite yeast roll. These were noted favorites in the Neiman Marcus catalog, and we had regular orders from that catalog alone. These rolls are light and airy, with just enough sweet potato. Make these at your next get-together and be prepared for someone to say, "May I have the recipe, please?"

MAKES: 24 ROLLS | PREP TIME: 2 1/2 HOURS | BAKE TIME: 12 TO 15 MINUTES

⅓ cup granulated sugar

½ cup warm water (110°F to 112°F)

1 (¼-ounce) packet dry active yeast

¾ cup canned sweet potatoes, mashed

3 tablespoons unsalted butter, melted

1 teaspoon salt

2 large eggs, beaten

3½ cups bread flour

¾ teaspoon baking powder

Cooking spray

1. In the bowl of a stand mixer, dissolve sugar in warm water and add yeast. Let bloom for 5 minutes.

2. Add the sweet potato puree, butter, salt, and beaten eggs. Using the paddle attachment, mix until well incorporated.

3. In a separate bowl, whisk together the bread flour and baking powder. Add flour mixture 1 cup at a time to the mixer bowl. Mix until dough clings to the paddle.

4. Place the dough on a floured surface and knead 4 to 5 times. Be careful not to over-knead.

5. Place the kneaded dough in a large oiled bowl and let rise for 1 hour or until doubled in size.

6. Prepare a 12-cup muffin pan with cooking spray.

7. Spray hands with pan spray, then punch down the dough and divide into fourths. Divide each fourth into 6 balls, 24 balls total. Place 2 balls into each cup of the prepared 12-cup muffin pan.

8. Cover the pan with a tea towel and let the rolls rise for 1 more hour.

9. Preheat the oven to 375°F while the rolls are rising. Once the rolls have finished rising, bake for 12 to 15 minutes or until golden brown.

10. Let cool slightly in the pan before removing. Serve warm or let the rolls cool completely before storing in an airtight container.

CHAPTER 2

soups
& SALADS

oups and salads can run the gamut from brunch staple to dinner entree. This chapter contains classic VeryVera recipes that could show up on a formal dinner table, in a summer picnic basket, or at your next ladies' luncheon.

SEASONINGS

Most of the recipes in this chapter call for dried herbs, but fresh can be substituted if you desire. To substitute fresh herbs for dry herbs, you will need to use triple the amount of fresh herbs, since dry herbs have a more concentrated flavor. If you are trying to decide if you should use fresh herbs or dry herbs, here is my suggestion: fresh herbs are better for garnishing or for adding at the end of a dish. Dry herbs are better for adding at the beginning of a dish, like when you are cooking soup.

SHELF LIFE

Unlike the soups and salads that you purchase at the grocery store, there have never been any preservatives used at VeryVera. Therefore, please note the 6-day shelf life on most of our recipes. These foods should always be stored in an airtight container to retain the level of quality.

FREEZING SOUPS

All the soups in this chapter will freeze well. The cream-based soups may separate during the thawing process, but they can easily be revived by putting the soup in a food processor with a little additional milk or cream. As with other recipes, always store and freeze soups in an airtight freezer container. The soups will expand when they are frozen, and if you do not use a freezer container, you might run the risk of your plastic container cracking.

SPECIALTY ITEMS

In the Seafood Bisque recipe (page 49), we use two ingredients that are more readily available to restaurants than home cooks. To re-create the authentic taste of the soup you enjoyed at VeryVera, we have made suggestions as to where to purchase these items. Specialty food stores have wonderful products and are a great place to look for items not typically sold at a grocery store. Amazon is also becoming a great resource for purchasing specialty food items.

SERVING SOUPS

Soup is intended to be served hot. The rule at VeryVera was that the bowl of soup had to be steaming when it arrived at the table.

GIFTS

Food always makes a great gift. In this chapter, two of my favorite things to gift are the Candied Pecans or Balsamic Vinaigrette found in the Pecan Crusted Chicken Salad (page 58). Both have a long shelf life and can be used in a variety of ways.

mama's egg salad

Just like Mama made it! What makes this egg salad special is the use of Durkee®, a sandwich spread found near the mustard at the store. You'll never open my refrigerator without finding a jar of Durkee! If you can't find it locally, yellow mustard and extra mayonnaise can be substituted. This egg salad was sold as a sandwich in the Café or in ½- or 1-pound containers in our case.

SERVES: 4 | PREP TIME: 45 MINUTES

8 LARGE EGGS

¼ CUP HELLMANN'S® MAYONNAISE (OR MORE IF YOU LIKE YOUR EGG SALAD LOOSER)

1 HEAPING TABLESPOON DURKEE® FAMOUS SAUCE

⅓ CUP SWEET PICKLE RELISH, DRAINED OF JUICE

¼ TEASPOON KOSHER SALT

¼ TEASPOON GROUND BLACK PEPPER

1. In a medium saucepan, cover the eggs completely with water and cover with the lid. Cook over high heat until the water comes to a complete boil and you can hear the eggs "dancing."

2. Turn off the heat and let the eggs sit for 20 minutes. At the end of that time, take off the lid and run cold water over the eggs until they are cool to the touch. Peel immediately.

3. Roughly chop the eggs. They should still be chunky.

4. Mix the remaining ingredients together in a large bowl.

5. Add the chopped eggs and gently mix until incorporated evenly.

6. Store in an airtight container in the refrigerator for up to 6 days.

FOR THE CAFÉ SANDWICH, SERVE THE EGG SALAD ON TOASTED WHITE BREAD WITH BACON AND TOMATO.

SEAFOOD BISQUE

This seafood bisque was dreamed up by one of my younger employees, Robert Gordon, at the Café and served every Friday. With tons of flavor, this decadent cream-based soup makes for a great weekend meal. Serve with crusty bread and you're good to go!

SERVES: 10 TO 12 | PREP TIME: 10 TO 15 MINUTES | COOK TIME: 50 MINUTES

¾ cup salted butter, divided

2¼ cups Vidalia onions, diced

1½ cups canned button mushrooms, drained and cut in half

½ cup all-purpose flour

2 tablespoons shrimp base*

1½ tablespoons lobster base*

4 cups whole milk

2 cups heavy cream

2 cups half & half

¾ teaspoon paprika

2¼ teaspoons granulated sugar

Cooked shrimp, for garnish

1. Melt ¼ cup of butter in a medium saucepan over medium heat.

2. Sauté the onions and mushrooms in the butter until the onions are translucent.

3. In a Dutch oven, melt the remaining ½ cup of butter. Add the flour and whisk until the flour has dissolved in the melted butter and a creamy, light brown paste (a roux) has formed.

4. Cook the roux until it is dark tan in color. Add the shrimp base and lobster base and mix well.

5. Stir in the milk slowly and let the mixture thicken until it looks like peanut butter.

6. Add the heavy cream and the half & half to the onions and mushrooms and heat through.

7. Slowly add the onion mixture to the roux mixture, then add the paprika. Let it come to a slow boil and then add the sugar.

8. Reduce to low heat and cook until the soup thickens, about 35 to 40 minutes.

9. Add shrimp to each serving as a garnish and a hearty addition.

NOTE: I USE FRESH LARGE SHRIMP SAUTÉED IN BUTTER AND CUT INTO BITE-SIZE CHUNKS. YOU CAN ALSO USE SMALL POPCORN-SIZE SHRIMP, ADDING 6 TO 8 TO A CUP OF SOUP OR 12 TO 14 TO A BOWL.

My husband and I are fortunate enough that our dock in Beaufort ends on top of a shrimp hole. One of our favorite things to do in Beaufort is to throw the cast net with the grandchildren.

Shrimp base and lobster base are available at specialty food stores. If you do not have a local specialty food store, check online at Amazon.com or an online specialty food store. Although it may require more work to find these ingredients, both add so much flavor to this soup and will give you enough to make this many times!

CRANBERRY ALMOND CHICKEN SALAD

In this not-so-traditional chicken salad, cranberries and curry powder mingle to provide depth of flavor. I recommend that you make this recipe a day ahead and let the flavors meld in the refrigerator overnight. The longer the chicken salad sits, the sweeter it becomes! This salad was served as a sandwich in our café or in ½- or 1-pound containers in our refrigerated case.

Serves: 8 to 10 (makes approximately 6 cups) | Prep Time: 25 to 30 minutes

2 ½ pounds boneless, skinless chicken breasts, raw

1 cup slivered almonds, toasted

1 to 1 ½ cups dried cranberries, to taste

1 cup celery, diced

1 cup green onions, diced

2 cups Hellmann's® mayonnaise

2 teaspoons curry powder

½ teaspoon white pepper

1 tablespoon fresh lemon juice

1. Boil the chicken breasts in salted water for about 10 to 12 minutes, until a thermometer inserted in the thickest breast registers 165°F.

2. Let the chicken cool and cut into ½-inch chunks.

3. In a large bowl, combine the chicken, almonds, cranberries, celery, and green onions.

4. In a separate bowl mix together the mayonnaise, seasonings, and lemon juice.

5. Mix the mayonnaise mixture into the chicken mixture until well blended. The color should be a very pale yellow.

6. Store in the refrigerator and allow the flavors to meld overnight.

7. Keep in an airtight container in the refrigerator for up to 6 days.

vera's signature chicken salad

Perfectly moist and full of flavor, this chicken salad is great on a bed of lettuce, in a sandwich, or by itself. Tarragon adds a licorice-like sweetness, and pecan pieces provide perfect textural balance. The Café menu sandwich was served on a croissant and chicken salad was also in our case in ½- or 1-pound containers. Don't start the weekend without this in your refrigerator.

SERVES: 8 TO 10 (MAKES APPROXIMATELY 6 CUPS) | PREP TIME: 25 TO 30 MINUTES

2 ½ POUNDS BONELESS, SKINLESS CHICKEN BREASTS, RAW

½ CUP PECAN PIECES

1 CUP GREEN ONIONS, SLICED

2 CUPS HELLMANN'S® MAYONNAISE

½ TEASPOON GROUND BLACK PEPPER

½ TEASPOON GARLIC SALT

½ TEASPOON ONION SALT

2 TABLESPOONS DRIED TARRAGON

1. Boil the chicken breasts in salted water for about 10 to 12 minutes until a thermometer inserted in the thickest breast registers 165°F.

2. Pulse the chicken in a food processor, leaving bigger pieces, or shred by hand for your desired consistency.

3. In a large bowl, combine the shredded chicken, pecan pieces, and green onions.

4. In a separate bowl, mix together the mayonnaise and seasonings.

5. Mix some of the mayonnaise mixture into the chicken mixture until well blended. Continue to incorporate the mayonnaise mixture until you have reached your desired consistency.

6. Store in the refrigerator and allow the flavors to meld overnight.

7. Keep in an airtight container in the refrigerator for up to 6 days.

GARDEN PATCH SOUP

At the Café, this recipe was the go-to for anyone looking for something light for Tuesday's lunch. This soup is brothy and full of colorful vegetables! Feel free to add any other veggies you have in your kitchen. The bow-tie pasta is only a garnish, but adding more will bulk up this soup if you're looking for something heartier.

SERVES: 10 TO 12 | PREP TIME: 20 MINUTES | COOK TIME: 1 HOUR AND 15 MINUTES

2 tablespoons salted butter

1½ teaspoons garlic, minced

1 cup yellow onions, diced

¾ cup celery, diced

8 cups chicken stock

½ teaspoon fresh rosemary

½ teaspoon fresh parsley

1 teaspoon kosher salt

½ teaspoon ground black pepper

1 teaspoon chicken base

1½ cups canned sliced mushrooms

1½ cups frozen sliced carrots

1½ cups frozen peas

1½ cups frozen corn

2½ cups raw chicken breast, diced

2 cups cooked bow-tie pasta, as garnish

1. Melt the butter in a large soup pot over medium heat.

2. Sauté the garlic, onions, and celery in butter until the onions are translucent.

3. Pour in the chicken stock, seasonings, chicken base, and all the vegetables.

4. Add the diced raw chicken.

5. Let the soup simmer, covered, for 1 hour or until it is hot and the chicken is cooked.

6. While the soup is simmering, cook the bow-tie pasta according to the directions on the package.

7. Serve the soup hot and garnish with bow-tie pasta.

Sandwiches

Vera's Signature Chicken Salad – chunks of white chicken lightly tossed in mayonnaise with pecans, green onion, and a hint of tarragon on a fresh croissant w/ leaf lettuce & choice of side. $6.50

Cranberry Chicken Salad – chunks of white chicken lightly tossed in mayonnaise with dried cranberries, green onions, almonds and a hint of curry on toasted whole wheat bread w/ lettuce, tomato & choice of side. $6.50

Tuna Melt – chunks of white tuna lightly tossed in mayonnaise with red onion, egg and celery on whole wheat with mushrooms and provolone cheese, lightly grilled and your choice of side. $6.50

The Grill – homemade pimento cheese on marbled rye with bacon and tomato, lightly grilled & your choice of side. $6.25

Momma's Egg Salad – southern egg salad on sourdough bread with bacon and tomato & choice of side. $6.25

Wraps

Chicken Caesar Wrap – marinated, grilled chicken with lettuce, tomatoes, and Parmesan cheese drizzled with a Caesar dressing in a flour tortilla, lightly grilled and your choice of side. $6.75

Bacon & Tomato Wrap – Our version of a BLT – homemade bacon tomato spread on a spinach wrap with sliced tomatoes, bacon, and lettuce served with your choice of a side. $7.00

Sides

Fresh Fruit
Chips
Pasta Salad
Side Salad (add $1)
Cup of Soup (add $1)

Salads

Pecan Crusted Chicken Salad – tender pecan crusted chicken breast on a bed of mixed greens with candied pecans, crumbled bleu cheese, dried cranberries, and mandarin oranges w/a balsamic vinaigrette served on the side. $7.75

Salad n' Salad – your choice of two of the following: Signature Chicken Salad, Cranberry Chicken Salad, Egg Salad, Pimento Cheese, Shrimp Pasta Salad, or Tuna Salad. Served with fresh fruit and a sour cream muffin. $8.25

Dressings – Balsamic Vinaigrette, Bleu Cheese, Honey Mustard, Ranch, Thousand Island, Light Italian, Poppy Seed

Soups

Cup	$2.75	Monday – Golden Summer Squash
Bowl	$4.00	Tuesday – Garden Patch
		Wednesday – Roasted Tomato Basil
		Thursday – Portabella Mushroom
		Friday – Seafood Bisque ($1.00 extra)

In the Mix

Soup n' Sandwich – cup of soup with your choice of any ½ sandwich or wrap. $6.75

Soup n' Salad – cup of soup with your choice of a scoop of Signature Chicken Salad, Cranberry Chicken Salad, Egg Salad, Pimento Cheese, Shrimp Pasta Salad, Tuna Salad, or a side Garden Salad. Add a side Pecan Crusted Chicken Salad or a side Summer Spinach Salad for $1 extra. $6.75

Quiche

Quiche of the Day – four cheese quiche prepared with daily topping and your choice of side. $7.25

Tomato Pie – Tomatoes, Parmesan & cheddar cheese, green onions, mayonnaise, salt, pepper, and basil in a flaky piecrust. Served with your choice of side. $7.50

Children's Menu $4.00

Grilled Cheese – served with choice of chips or fresh fruit and a cookie.
Peanut Butter and Jelly Sandwich – served with choice of chips or fruit and a cookie.

Southern Hospitality "No Tips Please"

POTATO HERB SOUP

There's nothing like a warm cup of potato soup on a chilly winter day, especially on a Monday, when this soup was served at the Café. This creamy soup recipe has everything needed to warm you to the core. I recommend a light chicken salad sandwich (page 50) to go with this hearty soup.

SERVES: 12 | PREP TIME: 25 MINUTES | COOK TIME: 1 HOUR AND 15 MINUTES

1 pound frozen potato cubes

1 stick salted butter, divided

¼ cup all-purpose flour

1 cup white onions, minced

½ teaspoon white pepper

¾ teaspoon garlic powder

¾ teaspoon garlic salt

2 tablespoons fresh parsley, roughly chopped, plus more for garnish

1 teaspoon chicken base

2 cups half & half

1 cup heavy cream

Kosher salt, to taste

Water, as desired

Fresh parsley, for garnish

1. Preheat the oven to 350°F.

2. Bake the frozen potato cubes until soft enough to squeeze by hand, about 10 minutes.

3. Use a potato masher to mash the potato cubes, leaving some of the potatoes chunky. Set aside.

4. In a large soup pot*, melt ¼ cup butter and add the flour, stirring constantly.

5. Cook the mixture until the flour is almost golden in color. (This would be considered a blonde roux.) Turn the heat down to low and stir occasionally.

6. Melt the remaining ¼ cup butter in a separate sauté pan.

7. Add the onions, white pepper, garlic powder, garlic salt, and parsley and cook until the onions are translucent.

8. While the onions cook, whisk the chicken base and the half & half together in a large liquid measuring cup.

9. Stir the half & half mixture and the heavy cream into the roux.

10. Once cooked, add the onion mixture to the stock pot and stir well.

11. Add the partially mashed potatoes to the stock pot.

12. Cook, covered, on low heat for 1 hour, stirring frequently, or use a double boiler to prevent the soup from scalding on the bottom of the pan.

13. Add water to thin the soup to the desired consistency.

14. Garnish with parsley and serve hot.

*NOTE: I RECOMMEND A LE CREUSET® PAN FOR THIS BECAUSE IT HAS A THICK BOTTOM AND WILL HELP PREVENT THE POTATOES FROM STICKING.

roasted tomato basil soup

You could set your watch by it—every Wednesday at the Café, the same group of Augustans would show up for tomato soup day. This soup is a labor of love, but the result is completely worth the effort. It's rich, full of flavor, and will fill your home with the delectable aroma of tomato and basil. Serve with a grilled pimento cheese sandwich (page 28) or a scoop of Vera's Signature Chicken Salad (page 50) for the perfect lunch.

SERVES: 6 TO 8 | PREP TIME: 25 MINUTES | COOK TIME: 1 HOUR AND 15 MINUTES

6 ROMA TOMATOES, SLICED IN HALF LENGTHWISE

2 TABLESPOONS GARLIC, MINCED

2 TABLESPOONS EXTRA-VIRGIN OLIVE OIL

KOSHER SALT, TO TASTE

GROUND BLACK PEPPER, TO TASTE

1 (14.5-OUNCE) CAN DICED TOMATOES, WITH JUICE

1½ CUPS FRESH BASIL, ROUGHLY CHOPPED

2 TABLESPOONS SALTED BUTTER

3 CUPS VIDALIA ONIONS, FINELY CHOPPED

½ CUP ALL-PURPOSE FLOUR

2 TEASPOONS GARLIC SALT

2 TABLESPOONS GRANULATED SUGAR

6½ CUPS CHICKEN BROTH

1 CUP WHOLE MILK

PARMESAN CHEESE, HAND-SHREDDED, FOR GARNISH

1. Preheat the oven to 325°F.

2. Slice the Roma tomatoes in half.

3. Toss the tomatoes with the garlic, oil, salt, and pepper.

4. Place the tomatoes on a parchment-lined sheet pan and roast in the preheated oven for 25 minutes.

5. When cooled, remove the skins of the tomatoes and discard.

6. Puree the peeled and roasted Roma tomatoes, canned diced tomatoes, and basil in a food processor until smooth.

7. In a large soup pot, melt the butter over medium heat and sauté the chopped onions until translucent.

8. Add the flour to the onions and stir, making sure there are no lumps.

9. Add the garlic salt, sugar, chicken broth, milk, and tomato puree to the pot and stir until thoroughly blended. Cook until heated through.

10. Serve hot with shredded Parmesan cheese as garnish.

BUTTERNUT SQUASH SOUP

If you love creamy soup, keep reading! Rich, creamy, and savory, this recipe is perfect for fall. Customers always came in on winter Tuesdays to cozy up with a mug of Butternut Squash Soup and enjoy the cool Augusta weather.

SERVES: 8 TO 10 | PREP TIME: 30 MINUTES | COOK TIME: 45 MINUTES

9 cups butternut squash, peeled and cubed (about 3 medium squashes)

¾ cup salted butter

½ cup all-purpose flour

2 tablespoons chicken base

1½ cups whole milk

⅛ teaspoon celery salt

⅛ teaspoon onion powder

⅛ teaspoon garlic powder

1½ teaspoons granulated sugar

1½ teaspoons salt

3 cups half & half

2½ cups applesauce

3 cups heavy cream

½ teaspoon rosemary, as garnish (optional)

1. Boil the squash in salted water until it is very soft, about 10 to 12 minutes. Drain.

2. Place the cooked squash in a food processor or blender to puree it. Set aside.

3. Melt the butter in a large pot over medium heat. Add the flour and whisk until the flour has dissolved in the melted butter and a creamy, light brown paste (roux) has formed.

4. Turn the heat to low and in a separate bowl, whisk the chicken base with the milk.

5. Back on low to medium heat, very slowly, add the chicken base mixture to the roux and stir until it thickens.

6. Add the celery salt, onion powder, garlic powder, sugar, salt, half & half, applesauce, and pureed butternut squash and stir until blended.

7. Slowly add the heavy cream and stir until well combined. Cook until heated through.

8. Serve hot. Garnish with rosemary if desired.

CUTTING A BUTTERNUT SQUASH

1. USING A LARGE KNIFE, CUT OFF A ¼-INCH SLICE FROM THE BOTTOM AND THE STEM.

2. PEEL THE BUTTERNUT SQUASH USING A VEGETABLE PEELER.

3. CUT THE SQUASH IN HALF LENGTHWISE. THIS IS DONE BEST BY SETTING THE SQUASH UPRIGHT ON A FLAT SURFACE.

4. USING A SPOON, SCRAPE OUT THE SEEDS FROM BOTH HALVES.

5. WITH THE CUT SIDE DOWN, CUT EACH SQUASH HALF INTO SLICES.

6. CUT EACH SLICE INTO CUBES.

pecan-crusted chicken salad

This is the one recipe in the book that we didn't ship from VeryVera. After first achieving popularity on our catering menu, it made its way to our Café favorites list when we opened the doors in 2004. More fondly referred to on the short-order side as PCC, it's going to be a favorite around your table, too. Turn this recipe into the VeryVera Café favorite "Vera's Salad" by leaving off the pecan-crusted chicken.

MAKES: 6 SALADS | PREP TIME: 40 MINUTES | COOK TIME: 15 TO 20 MINUTES

SALAD

2 CUPS PECANS

4 TABLESPOONS ALL-PURPOSE FLOUR

6 BONELESS, SKINLESS CHICKEN BREASTS

KOSHER SALT, TO TASTE

GROUND BLACK PEPPER, TO TASTE

1 CUP BUTTERMILK

3 CUPS SPRING MIX LETTUCE BLEND

⅓ CUP CANDIED PECANS (PAGE 60)

¾ CUP BLUE CHEESE CRUMBLES

¾ CUP DRIED CRANBERRIES

¾ CUP MANDARIN ORANGES

BALSAMIC VINAIGRETTE

BALSAMIC VINAIGRETTE

3 TABLESPOONS BALSAMIC VINEGAR

3 TABLESPOONS HELLMANN'S® MAYONNAISE

2 TABLESPOONS WATER

2 CLOVES GARLIC, PRESSED

1 TEASPOON DIJON MUSTARD

2 TEASPOONS DARK BROWN SUGAR

3 TABLESPOONS EXTRA-VIRGIN OLIVE OIL

KOSHER SALT, TO TASTE

GROUND BLACK PEPPER, TO TASTE

1. Preheat the oven to 325°F.

2. Grind the pecans in a food processor until they are the consistency of cornmeal.

3. Add the flour to the food processor and pulse to mix. Pour the flour mixture into a pie plate.

4. Pat the chicken breasts dry and season on both sides with salt and pepper.

5. Pour the buttermilk into its own pie plate.

6. Dip each chicken breast in the buttermilk to coat, then coat in the pecan mixture.

7. Bake on a parchment-lined baking sheet for 15 to 20 minutes, or until a thermometer inserted in the thickest breast registers 165°F. Remove from the oven and allow to cool.

8. Once the breasts have cooled, slice thinly, about ¼ inch thick.

9. Arrange the lettuce on salad plates, and sprinkle the pecans, blue cheese, cranberries, and oranges on top of each salad.

10. Place the chicken on top of the lettuce and serve with balsamic vinaigrette.

balsamic vinaigrette

1. Blend the balsamic vinegar, mayonnaise, water, garlic, mustard, and brown sugar together in a blender.

2. Slowly add the olive oil until all ingredients are mixed well.

3. Salt and pepper the dressing to taste.

TIP: TO SEE HOW VERYVERA INCORPORATES THIS SALAD INTO A MEAL, SEE OUR MENU PLANNING SECTION (PAGE 172).

CONTINUED ON 60

CONTINUED FROM 58

candied pecans

CANDIED PECANS

½ CUP WATER

½ CUP GRANULATED SUGAR

2½ CUPS PECAN HALVES

1. Preheat the oven to 325°F and line a sheet pan with parchment paper.

2. In a large saucepan, bring the water to a boil over medium heat.

3. Add the granulated sugar and let it dissolve.

4. Once the sugar is dissolved, pour in the pecans and stir.

5. Let the pecans cook, stirring every few minutes. The liquid will begin to thicken.

6. When most of the liquid has cooked out, the pecans will be shiny and sticky. Remove from the cooktop.

7. Spread the pecans on the prepared sheet pan.

NOTE: EXTRA PECANS CAN BE STORED IN HEAVY RESEALABLE BAGS. THEY ALSO MAKE A GREAT GIFT.

8. Place in the oven and bake for 8 to 10 minutes or until they are not shiny and look frosty.

9. Let the pecans cool and break apart before serving on the salad.

Tuna salad

The "chicken of the sea" has its own salad, too! Fresh lemon juice brightens up this salad and cuts the creaminess of the mayonnaise. I also like the touch of a little bit of sugar to balance the fishy flavor of the tuna. In the Café, it was served as a Tuna Melt and was available in our case in ½- or 1-pound containers.

SERVES: 8 | PREP TIME: 20 MINUTES

2 (12-OUNCE, 9-OUNCE DRY WEIGHT) CANS CHICKEN OF THE SEA® CHUNK LIGHT TUNA (IN WATER)

4 HARD-BOILED LARGE EGGS, DICED

⅓ CUP CELERY, DICED

⅓ CUP RED ONION, DICED

½ TO ¾ CUP HELLMANN'S® MAYONNAISE, TO TASTE

2 TEASPOONS GRANULATED SUGAR, OR MORE TO TASTE

COARSELY GROUND BLACK PEPPER, TO TASTE

1 TABLESPOON FRESH LEMON JUICE

1. In a large bowl, mix together the tuna, eggs, celery, and red onion.

2. In a separate bowl, combine the mayonnaise, sugar, black pepper, and lemon juice. Mix until well blended.

3. Pour the sauce into the tuna mixture and mix well.

4. Serve cold.

5. Keep in an airtight container in the refrigerator for up to 6 days.

TUNA MELT: TOASTED SOURDOUGH BREAD WITH TUNA SALAD AND PROVOLONE CHEESE.

portabella mushroom soup

Portabellas are some of the largest, meatiest mushrooms. This soup is so rich and velvety, you won't even think about the fact that it doesn't contain meat. This soup had our Café packed on Thursdays! Due to the richness, I recommend a salad accompaniment, like the Pecan-Crusted Chicken Salad (page 58), instead of a sandwich.

SERVES: 4 TO 6 | PREP TIME: 30 MINUTES | COOK TIME: 40 TO 45 MINUTES

4 TABLESPOONS SALTED BUTTER, DIVIDED

2 CUPS PORTABELLA MUSHROOMS, CLEANED AND DICED

¾ CUP GREEN ONIONS, DICED

2 TABLESPOONS ALL-PURPOSE FLOUR

2 TEASPOONS CHICKEN BASE

½ CUP WHOLE MILK

½ CUP HALF & HALF

1 CUP HEAVY CREAM

FRESHLY CRACKED BLACK PEPPER, TO TASTE

WATER, AS DESIRED

1. Melt 1 tablespoon of butter in a soup pot.

2. Sauté the mushrooms and onions in the melted butter.

3. In a separate pot, melt the remaining butter and add the flour, whisking constantly until a roux forms. Turn down the heat to low and stir occasionally.

4. In a liquid measuring cup, mix the chicken base and milk with a whisk.

5. Turn the heat back to medium and add the chicken-base mixture to the roux, stirring constantly until it thickens. I like to use my flat-edge wooden spoon so I can feel the bottom of the pan and make sure the thickening soup is not scalding on the bottom. The roux will be thick.

6. Remove the pot from the heat.

7. Add the roux, half & half, and heavy cream to the mushrooms and onions in the soup pot.

8. Cook on low heat for 35 to 40 minutes, or until the soup thickens. Serve hot. If the soup becomes too thick, loosen with water.

CHAPTER 3

vegetables

& SIDES

$\mathcal{H}$ow many times have you asked, or been asked, "What can I bring?" This chapter is the answer to that question. Whether you're rounding out *your* own dinner menu or trying not to show up empty-handed at a potluck, turn to one of the tried-and-true recipes that sustained VeryVera customers for years!

SELECTING FRESH VEGETABLES

There is a time and place for frozen vegetables. They are wonderful to use in soup or for weeknight side dishes, but when it comes to recipes where the vegetable is the star, there's no substitute for fresh. I love going to my local produce market to pick up vegetables in season. Typically, locally sourced vegetables are much fresher because there is less time between harvesting and purchasing.

HAND-SHREDDING CHEESE

I always shred my own cheese when a recipe calls for shredded cheese. This is fresher, and you can choose the size of the shred depending on the recipe. This is also the more cost-effective choice.

MINCED GARLIC

When it comes to minced garlic, always opt for freshly minced cloves over the jarred variety. Jarred minced garlic does not contain the same purity of flavor that freshly minced garlic does. If you feel comfortable with your knife skills, you can mince garlic with a chef's knife. If you'd prefer, you can choose to use a garlic press. This garlic will be a very fine mince, almost paste-like.

SUBSTITUTIONS

Substitutions are how you create *your* version of the recipe. To be authentic to the VeryVera Brand, I recommend following the recipe, but once you have mastered it, start looking for ways to tweak it. Make the VeryVera recipes your family recipes by keeping them the same or adding your twist. A few substitutions I often make are replacing olive oil with a bit of bacon grease for a Southern twist and adding in red pepper flakes for color and a kick!

GIFTS

I always thought a great side dish made the perfect bereavement gift. There are great disposable pans or clear plastic bowls that no one needs to return. You can always count on fried chicken, ham, or turkey, but who is going to remember to bring a side to go with it?

parmesan squash casserole

*This casserole screams "autumn" to me because it's perfect for holiday gatherings.
I also love making this in the summer when golden squashes are ripe on the vine.
Green peppers break up the rich cheesiness of a traditional casserole. The recipe calls
for bread crumbs, but I also like to use crushed Ritz® crackers. I prefer steaming the
squash over boiling it, as it will preserve its color, texture, and nutrients.*

SERVES: 8 TO 10 | PREP TIME: 30 TO 35 MINUTES | COOK TIME: 30 MINUTES

2 POUNDS YELLOW SQUASH

1¼ CUPS HELLMANN'S®
MAYONNAISE

3 LARGE EGGS, BEATEN

½ TEASPOON KOSHER SALT

½ TEASPOON GROUND BLACK
PEPPER

¾ CUP PANKO BREAD CRUMBS

2 CUPS PARMESAN CHEESE,
HAND-SHREDDED

¼ CUP GREEN BELL PEPPER,
CHOPPED (OPTIONAL)

¾ CUP GREEN ONIONS,
CHOPPED

1. Preheat the oven to 325°F and grease a 7 x 11-inch pan with cooking spray.

2. Slice the yellow squash into 1-inch pieces.

3. Place a steam basket in a Dutch oven over boiling water and steam for about 10 minutes, or until the squash is fork tender.

4. Mix together the mayonnaise, eggs, salt, pepper, bread crumbs, and Parmesan cheese.

5. Stir in the green peppers and green onions.

6. Add the yellow squash last and mix until well incorporated.

7. Pour into the prepared pan and place in the oven.

8. Bake for 30 minutes or until the casserole bubbles and the top is lightly browned.

NOTE: LIFELONG FRIENDS BILL GIBBS AND PAT COLLINS ATE LUNCH TOGETHER ONCE A WEEK AT THE CAFÉ. ONE OF THEIR FAVORITE PARTS OF THE EXPERIENCE WAS THE BULLETIN BOARD THAT WE CHANGED OUT MONTHLY. THEY SAID IT REMINDED THEM OF ELEMENTARY SCHOOL.

TOMATO PIE

Tomato Pie is the savory king of the pie family—the rooster, you might say. Creamy, savory, flaky, and hearty, this pie works at any time of year. Roma tomatoes hold up perfectly through baking and maintain their structure without falling apart. This popular VeryVera favorite sold out every day.

MAKES: 1 PIE, SERVES 6 TO 8 PEOPLE | PREP TIME: 20 TO 30 MINUTES | COOK TIME: 30 MINUTES

3 or 4 Roma tomatoes, sliced ½-inch thick

Salt, to taste

Ground black pepper, to taste

½ cup Parmesan cheese, hand-shredded

1 cup sharp cheddar cheese, hand-shredded

1 cup Hellmann's® mayonnaise

1 frozen pie shell

¼ cup green onions, sliced

¼ cup fresh basil, chopped

1. Preheat the oven to 400°F.

2. Place the sliced tomatoes on paper towels. Sprinkle with salt and pepper.

3. Mix both cheeses and mayonnaise together.

4. Place the first layer of tomatoes in the pie shell, completely covering the bottom. Cut a tomato slice in half to completely cover the bottom if need be. Sprinkle with a third of the green onions and basil, and spread a third of the cheese mixture on top.

5. Repeat with two more layers. On the final layer, be sure to let the tomatoes show through the cheese.

6. Bake for 30 minutes or until the cheese is melted and bubbling.

NOTE: FOR LEFTOVERS, SLICE AND PLATE. HEAT INDIVIDUAL SLICES IN THE MICROWAVE IN 30-SECOND INTERVALS UNTIL HEATED THROUGH.

SOUTHERN SAGE AND CORNBREAD DRESSING

Are you ready for your next Thanksgiving staple? Plenty of VeryVera customers have ordered this dressing for their Thanksgiving meal, but it's so simple to make! This dressing is chunky, moist, and the perfect complement to your Thanksgiving bird or with a grilled chicken breast or pork tenderloin during the week.

SERVES: 8 TO 10 | PREP TIME: 30 TO 35 MINUTES | COOK TIME: 20 MINUTES

½ (1-pound) loaf sourdough bread, thickly sliced

7 ounces (about 3 cups) Pepperidge Farm® Classic Cornbread Stuffing Mix

1 stick unsalted butter

½ cup Vidalia onions, sliced

¼ leek, thinly sliced

½ cup celery, chopped

4 ounces white button mushrooms, diced

¼ teaspoon salt

¼ teaspoon ground black pepper

½ teaspoon ground sage

¼ teaspoon poultry seasoning

2 to 3 cups chicken broth

1. Preheat the oven to 350°F.

2. Into a large bowl, tear the sourdough slices into 1-inch cubes.

3. Add the cornbread stuffing mix.

4. In a medium sauté pan over medium heat, melt the butter.

5. Sauté the onions, leeks, celery, and button mushrooms until the onions are translucent.

6. Add the seasonings and stir well.

7. Add the sautéed vegetables to the bread mixture and lightly toss to distribute the vegetables evenly.

8. Pour in the chicken broth and stir with a wooden spoon until the bread mixture is moist enough to stick together.

9. Place in a seasoned cast-iron skillet and bake for 20 minutes.

BROCCOLI SALAD

When we opened the Café in 2004, cold broccoli salad was very trendy and new. Wanting to incorporate new with our classic Southern, this became our standard side to our sandwiches. I recommend selecting a whole head of broccoli and cutting the florets yourself.

SERVES: 4 TO 6 | PREP TIME: 15 TO 20 MINUTES

1 large head raw broccoli (approximately 6 cups broccoli florets)

1 cup bacon, cooked (approximately 6 to 8 slices)

1 small red onion, diced

1 cup dried cranberries (Craisins®)

1 cup Hellmann's® mayonnaise

¼ cup white wine vinegar

½ cup granulated sugar

½ teaspoon freshly cracked black pepper

1. Cut off the broccoli stems and halve broccoli spears. Place in a large bowl.

2. Crumble the cooked bacon over the broccoli.

3. Add the onion and dried cranberries.

4. In a separate bowl, mix together the mayonnaise, vinegar, and sugar.

5. Pour ¾ of the dressing over the broccoli and add freshly cracked pepper. Mix until well incorporated.

6. Let the salad sit in the refrigerator overnight for best results.

7. Pour the remaining dressing over the salad right before serving.

POTATO SALAD

This classic Southern side should never be left off the picnic table. In my house, it should always be on the menu when the family gathers, and our Café customers couldn't eat lunch without it. My two cents' worth: serve warm and use Hellmann's® mayonnaise.

SERVES: 4 TO 6 | PREP TIME: 15 TO 20 MINUTES

2½ pounds russet potatoes

⅓ cup Vidalia onion, diced

4 large eggs, hard-cooked

2 tablespoons sweet pickle relish

1 teaspoon celery seeds

1½ teaspoons salt

½ teaspoon ground black pepper

½ to ¾ cup Hellmann's® mayonnaise (depending on personal preference)

1. Peel, rinse, and chop the potatoes into ½-inch cubes.

2. Put the potato pieces in a pot of salted water and bring to a boil. Reduce heat and cook until potatoes are fork tender.

3. Drain the potatoes in a colander.

4. Place the diced onions in a large bowl, then add the hot potato cubes.

5. Chop the hard-cooked eggs and place on top of potatoes.

6. Add the relish, celery seeds, salt, and pepper to hot potatoes and let sit until slightly cooled.

7. Add the mayonnaise and stir until well blended.

8. Preferably, serve warm.

PICTURED ON 71

PASTA SALAD WITH LEMON BASIL DRESSING

VeryVera Café was noted for its delicious sandwiches with a variety of specialty sides. The number one choice was our Pasta Salad. Lemon juice and basil cut the creamy mayonnaise to keep it light. Add grilled chicken or shrimp and make this a summer entrée salad.

SERVES: 4 TO 6 | PREP TIME: 30 MINUTES

1 (16-ounce) box medium pasta shells

1 cup frozen peas, thawed

1 cup black olives, sliced

1 medium sweet red pepper, diced

⅓ cup scallions, diced

Salt, to taste

Ground black pepper, to taste

2 cups Hellmann's® mayonnaise

¼ cup fresh lemon juice

½ cup fresh basil leaves, minced

2 cloves garlic, minced

1. Cook the pasta according to package instructions, drain, rinse, and cool.

2. Combine the pasta, peas, olives, red pepper, scallions, salt, and pepper in a large bowl and refrigerate.

3. Combine the remaining ingredients in a small bowl and mix well.

4. Pour half of the dressing over the salad, toss well, and store the remaining dressing.

5. Refrigerate the salad overnight.

6. Pour the remaining dressing over the pasta salad and mix well before serving.

7. Garnish with whole black olives and sliced red peppers.

CREAMED SPINACH

I was never a fan of cooked spinach until my mother-in-law introduced me to adding nutmeg. I love the cozy warmness of nutmeg combined with the nuttiness of Parmesan cheese.

SERVES: 8 TO 10 | PREP TIME: 15 TO 20 MINUTES | COOK TIME: 15 MINUTES

5 (10-ounce) boxes chopped frozen spinach

3 tablespoons salted butter

¾ cup extra virgin olive oil

2 teaspoons garlic, minced

1½ cups heavy cream

1 teaspoon ground nutmeg

½ cup Parmesan cheese, hand-shredded

1½ teaspoons salt

⅓ teaspoon ground black pepper

1. Thaw the frozen spinach, place into a colander, and let it drain well. Press out as much liquid as possible.

2. Heat the butter and oil in a large skillet over medium-high heat, then add garlic.

3. Cook, stirring frequently, until light brown, then add spinach.

4. Add the cream and nutmeg and cook until it reduces slightly, about 5 minutes.

5. Add the Parmesan cheese and season with salt and pepper.

6. Cook until the spinach is hot, about 5 more minutes, and serve.

SWEET POTATO CASSEROLE WITH PRALINE TOPPING

Every Thanksgiving, the debate always returns: streusel topping or marshmallow topping for those creamy sweet potatoes? My brown sugar and pecan topping errs on the side of streusel, but I'd rather not plant my flag on one side or the other.

SERVES: 6 TO 8 | PREP TIME: 1 HOUR AND 10 MINUTES | COOK TIME: 45 MINUTES

FILLING

3 large sweet potatoes (approximately 4 cups cooked)

½ cup granulated sugar

½ tablespoon pure vanilla extract

1 large egg

½ cup half and half

PRALINE TOPPING

⅔ cup self-rising flour

½ cup brown sugar, packed

½ cup pecans, chopped

½ cup unsalted butter, melted

½ teaspoon ground cinnamon

1. Preheat the oven to 350°F.

2. Bake the whole sweet potatoes for 1 hour.

3. While the potatoes are baking, combine all the ingredients for the praline topping; set aside.

4. Remove the baked sweet potatoes from the oven. When they are cool enough to touch, remove the skins and mash the pulp in a large bowl. If you want a creamier mixture, pulse in a food processor.

5. Add the remaining filling ingredients to the sweet potatoes and mix until well blended. Scoop into an 8 x 8-inch dish and set aside.

6. Dollop the topping evenly over the casserole mixture. It is sticky, but it can most easily be distributed by hand.

7. Bake for 30 minutes or until the topping is golden brown and the casserole is bubbling.

TIP: IF YOU MAKE THIS FOR EASTER, TRY USING MULTICOLORED MARSHMALLOWS, AND CHILDREN PRESENT MIGHT BE MORE INCLINED TO PARTAKE!

macaroni and cheese

We had a contest at VeryVera to create a Macaroni and Cheese recipe that was truly Southern while maintaining a certain level of sophistication. Four different cheeses make this recipe the creamiest, cheesiest macaroni and cheese you've ever tasted. Panko bread crumbs add crunch and texture without stealing moisture from the rich, cheesy pasta underneath.

SERVES: 8 TO 10 | PREP TIME: 30 MINUTES | COOK TIME: 25 TO 30 MINUTES

1 POUND MACARONI

⅓ CUP MONTEREY JACK CHEESE, HAND-SHREDDED

⅓ CUP HAVARTI CHEESE, HAND-SHREDDED

6 OUNCES VELVEETA CHEESE, CUT INTO CUBES

1¾ CUPS SHARP CHEDDAR CHEESE (RESERVE ¾ CUP FOR TOPPING), HAND-SHREDDED

1 STICK SALTED BUTTER (RESERVE 1 TABLESPOON)

2¾ CUPS HEAVY CREAM

1 LARGE EGG

¾ TEASPOON KOSHER SALT

⅛ TEASPOON GROUND BLACK PEPPER

1 CUP PANKO BREAD CRUMBS

1. Preheat the oven to 325°F and prepare an 8 x 8-inch pan with cooking spray.

2. Boil the macaroni according to the package directions until al dente, being careful not to overcook. Drain the cooked macaroni.

3. In a large bowl, mix together the first 3 cheeses, plus 1 cup of shredded cheddar. Then add 7 tablespoons of the butter and the heavy cream.

4. Pour the hot macaroni over the cheese mixture, cover, and let sit until the cheese is soft but not completely melted.

5. In a separate large bowl, beat together the egg, salt, and pepper. Add this to the macaroni mixture and combine thoroughly.

6. Pour the macaroni mixture into the prepared pan. Top with the reserved ¾ cup shredded cheddar and panko bread crumbs, and dot with the remaining 1 tablespoon of butter.

7. Bake for 25 to 30 minutes or until golden brown.

NOTE: IF MAKING A DAY AHEAD, STOP AFTER ADDING THE MACARONI MIXTURE TO THE CASSEROLE DISH. JUST BEFORE HEATING, TOP WITH CHEESE, PANKO, AND BUTTER, BAKE, AND SERVE WHEN READY.

CHAPTER 4

main
DISHES

$\mathcal{W}$ ho doesn't get excited over talk of a good entrée? This chapter contains some staples from my Café days that span breakfast, lunch, and dinner. Show up to a potluck with one of these main dishes and be prepared to be the center of attention!

PAN PREPARATION

For all the recipes in this chapter, we recommend PAM® cooking spray for consistency, quality, and ease in cleaning. Unless covered baking is suggested in the recipe, all baking will be uncovered. When covered baking is suggested, the shiny side of aluminum foil should be facing down on the covered dish. My final suggestion for clean baking is to place the casserole dishes on a sheet pan. This will ensure that if anything bubbles over, you won't have to clean your oven, and it makes getting the dish in and out of the oven much easier.

HAND-SHREDDING CHEESE

I always shred my own cheese when a recipe calls for shredded cheese. This is fresher, and you can choose the size of the shred depending on the recipe. This is also the more cost-effective choice. Most of the recipes that use cheese call for hand-shredded cheese. This will be long strips of cheese when you use the standard side of a box grater. Hand-grated cheese will be finer. Grated cheese can be done on the fine setting of a box grater or using a rotary grater.

TOOLS AND EQUIPMENT

• **Sturdy rubber spatula**—These are just great for mixing and folding all types of ingredients.

• **Good wooden spoon**—A good wooden spoon has a medium handle length, and it is thin enough so you can "feel" in the pan when you are stirring. It is such a versatile tool!

• **Wire whisk**—There's nothing like a heavy-duty wire whisk.

baked french toast

As a child, French toast was my favorite weekend breakfast, taking the top spot over pancakes. Then, when my sons were growing up, it continued to be the house favorite, but the extensive prep relegated it to weekends or holidays only. We created this version at VeryVera to give everyone his or her favorite breakfast treat any time.

SERVES: 4 | PREP TIME: 20 MINUTES | COOK TIME: 25 MINUTES

1 CUP HEAVY CREAM

⅔ CUP WHOLE MILK

4 LARGE EGGS

¼ TEASPOON GROUND CINNAMON

⅛ TEASPOON GROUND NUTMEG

½ TEASPOON PURE VANILLA EXTRACT

⅛ TEASPOON SALT

8 SLICES FRENCH BREAD, SLICED ¾ INCH THICK

1 CUP DARK BROWN SUGAR, PACKED

⅓ CUP GRANULATED SUGAR

2 TABLESPOONS ALL-PURPOSE FLOUR

¼ CUP MAPLE SYRUP, PLUS ADDITIONAL FOR TOPPING

¾ CUP PECANS, CHOPPED

CONFECTIONERS' SUGAR FOR TOPPING

1. Preheat the oven to 325°F.

2. In a large bowl, mix together the heavy cream, milk, eggs, cinnamon, nutmeg, vanilla, and salt.

3. Grease a 9 x 13-inch pan with cooking spray.

4. Pour ½ cup of the egg mixture in the bottom of the pan.

5. Soak the bread in egg mixture for 2 minutes, pressing down on the bread to absorb the liquid.

6. While the bread is soaking, mix the brown sugar, granulated sugar, and flour in a separate bowl.

7. Transfer the soaked bread to a parchment-lined baking sheet.

8. Sprinkle the soaked bread slices generously with the sugar mixture, flip over, and repeat.

9. Stack the slices at a slant across the 9 x 13-inch pan and push them together so they all fit in the pan.

10. Pour the remaining egg mixture over the bread slices.

11. Drizzle the bread slices with the maple syrup and sprinkle with the pecans.

12. Bake for 25 minutes, uncovered.

13. Serve warm and garnish with confectioners' sugar and additional maple syrup, if you like.

BREAKFAST CASSEROLE

A family favorite, this Breakfast Casserole finds itself at the table for every celebratory morning occasion, but it should be made the night before. It includes all the breakfast staples, and the little bit of dry mustard adds a tangy flavor and cuts through some of the richness of the dish. Everyone will be begging for Breakfast Casserole, which is simple to prepare but sure to please.

SERVES: 10 TO 12 | PREP TIME: 20 MINUTES | COOK TIME: 45 MINUTES

6 slices white bread

1 pound pork sausage (mild or hot, depending on preference)

2 tablespoons salted butter

5 large eggs

2 cups half & half

¼ teaspoon dry mustard

2 cups sharp cheddar cheese, hand-shredded

1. Tear the bread into ½-inch pieces and place in the bottom of a greased 9 x 13-inch casserole dish.

2. Cook the sausage and drain the excess fat.

3. Melt the butter in the microwave and pour over the bread pieces.

4. Sprinkle the cooked sausage over the bread and butter.

5. In a large liquid measuring cup, mix together the eggs, half & half, and dry mustard.

6. Pour the egg mixture over the bread and sausage.

7. Sprinkle the cheddar cheese over the top of the casserole and refrigerate overnight.

8. Remove from the refrigerator and preheat the oven to 350°F.

9. Bake uncovered for 45 minutes.

10. Serve immediately.

Here's what's cookin': Sausage - Egg Casserole

Recipe from the kitchen of: Lyn Hunt   Serves: 4-5

1 lb. bulk sausage
6 slices white bread, crusts removed
softened butter (3 Tbs)
1½ c. shredded Longhorn cheese
5 eggs
2 c. Half + Half
1 tsp. salt
1 tsp. dry mustard

Cook sausage -
Drain. Set asi
spread bread

chicken and wild rice casserole

One of my products sold at Costco, Chicken and Wild Rice Casserole is a crowd pleaser. It's a classic comfort food and one that your family and friends will be asking you to make again and again. Water chestnuts add an interesting crunch, but feel free to leave them out if you would prefer a more classic preparation.

SERVES: 6 TO 8 | PREP TIME: 40 TO 45 MINUTES | BAKE TIME: 25 TO 30 MINUTES

CASSEROLE

2 POUNDS RAW, BONELESS, SKINLESS CHICKEN BREASTS (4 CUPS COOKED AND DICED CHICKEN)

SALT

1 BOX UNCLE BEN'S® LONG GRAIN AND WILD RICE BLEND, ORIGINAL RECIPE (DO NOT USE SEASONING POUCH)

2 CUPS CHICKEN BROTH

1 CUP CELERY, DICED

1 CUP SLICED WATER CHESTNUTS, CUT IN HALF

1 CUP FROZEN AND THAWED GREEN PEAS

SAUCE

¾ TEASPOON SALT

⅛ TEASPOON GARLIC SALT

¾ TEASPOON ONION POWDER

1½ CUPS HELLMANN'S® MAYONNAISE

2 TABLESPOONS FRESH LEMON JUICE

1 TABLESPOON WORCESTERSHIRE SAUCE

1 TEASPOON DIJON MUSTARD

¼ TEASPOON FINELY GROUND BLACK PEPPER

¾ CUP SHARP CHEDDAR CHEESE, HAND-SHREDDED

OPTIONAL TOPPING

2 TABLESPOONS COOKED AND CRUMBLED BACON

1. Lightly salt the chicken and boil for 10 minutes (the chicken will still be slightly raw). Dice into bite-sized pieces.

2. Preheat the oven to 350°F and grease a 7 x 11-inch dish with cooking spray.

3. In a large pot, cook the wild rice with the chicken broth according to package directions.

4. Combine the cooked chicken, cooked wild rice, celery, water chestnuts, and peas. Mix well.

5. In a separate bowl, mix all the sauce ingredients together.

6. Add the sauce to the chicken mixture. Mix well.

7. Pour the casserole mixture into the prepared 7 x 11-inch dish.

8. Top with the bacon if desired.

9. Bake the casserole for 25 to 30 minutes or until hot and bubbling.

NOTE: TO FREEZE FOR LATER USE, DO NOT COOK THE ASSEMBLED CASSEROLE. TO SERVE, TAKE THE CASSEROLE DIRECTLY FROM THE FREEZER TO THE OVEN AND INCREASE THE COOK TIME TO 50 MINUTES.

CHICKEN POT PIE

When my boys were young, I always kept a few fully prepared chicken pot pies in the freezer for busy evenings when I ran out of time to cook a meal from scratch. To keep from having "guilty mom syndrome," I made up a jingle about the menu—"Chicken Pot Pie and I don't care"—to get the children excited about dinner. This version needs no special jingle, just a few extra minutes to make it. This is great for company, family dinner, or to take to a friend.

SERVES: 8 TO 10 | PREP TIME: 40 MINUTES | COOK TIME: 35 TO 40 MINUTES

1 package Pillsbury®
refrigerated pie crusts
(2 pie crusts)

⅓ cup salted butter

⅓ cup white onion, diced

⅓ cup celery, diced

⅓ cup all-purpose flour

½ teaspoon salt

¼ teaspoon ground black pepper

¼ teaspoon rubbed sage

1½ cups chicken broth

⅔ cup whole milk

2 to 3 cups frozen mixed vegetables (corn, peas, carrots), thawed

4 cups cooked chicken (1 rotisserie chicken), hand-shredded

1. Preheat the oven to 425°F.

2. Line a 9-inch deep-dish pie pan with 1 pie crust. Set aside.

3. In a large saucepan over medium heat, sauté the butter, onions, and celery until tender.

4. Add the flour, salt, pepper, and sage and whisk until bubbly.

5. Gradually whisk in the chicken broth and milk, stirring constantly until bubbly and thickened.

6. Add the vegetables and chicken to the sauce and mix. Remove from the heat.

7. Spoon the chicken-and-vegetable mixture into the crust-lined pie dish.

8. Top with the second crust and flute or pinch the edges together. Cut slits in several places before baking. (I also recommend a lattice crust, as pictured.)

9. Place the pie dish on a sheet pan and place in the oven.

10. Bake for 35 to 40 minutes or until golden brown.

11. Let stand for 5 minutes before serving.

shrimp and crawfish

Calling all seafood lovers! The level of spiciness in this creamy dish is adjustable for all tastes. This recipe will fill your home with savory aromas that will have the neighbors wanting to invite themselves over. Feel free to sauté your shrimp rather than bake it.

SERVES: 10 TO 12 | PREP TIME: 45 MINUTES TO 1 HOUR | COOK TIME: 20 MINUTES

1 POUND PEELED AND DEVEINED 51/60 SHRIMP

½ POUND DRY FETTUCCINE NOODLES, BROKEN IN HALF

2 TABLESPOONS EXTRA-VIRGIN OLIVE OIL, DIVIDED

½ STICK UNSALTED BUTTER

½ CUP WHITE ONION, DICED

¼ CUP GREEN BELL PEPPER, DICED

¼ CUP CELERY, DICED

½ TEASPOON GARLIC, MINCED

½ CUP ROTEL® ORIGINAL DICED TOMATOES & GREEN CHILIES, WITH JUICE

¼ CUP DRIED PARSLEY, PLUS MORE FOR GARNISH

½ (10½-OUNCE) CAN CREAM OF SHRIMP SOUP

1 CUP SHARP CHEDDAR CHEESE, HAND-SHREDDED

1 CUP MONTEREY JACK CHEESE, HAND-SHREDDED

¼ TEASPOON GROUND BLACK PEPPER

¾ TEASPOON TONY CHACHERE'S® CREOLE SEASONING

½ POUND COOKED CRAWFISH TAIL MEAT

PARMESAN CHEESE, HAND-GRATED FOR GARNISH

1. Preheat the oven to 325°F and grease a 9 x 13-inch pan with cooking spray.

2. Bake the shrimp on a parchment-lined sheet pan in the oven for 5 minutes. Set aside.

3. Cook the noodles in boiling water with 1 tablespoon of olive oil.

4. Once the noodles are fully cooked, drain, and toss them with the remaining olive oil. Set aside.

5. Melt the butter in a Dutch oven over medium heat.

6. Sauté the onion, bell pepper, celery, and garlic over medium heat for 15 minutes or until the onions are translucent.

7. Add the tomatoes and parsley to the sautéed vegetables and cook for another 5 minutes.

8. Add the soup, both cheeses, and seasonings.

9. Let the mixture simmer until the cheese is melted.

10. Add the noodles, shrimp, and crawfish to the sauce. Mix until well incorporated.

11. Place in the greased 9 x 13-inch pan, cover with foil, and bake for 20 minutes or until hot.

12. Garnish with grated Parmesan cheese and parsley.

NOTE: THIS WAS A GO-TO FAVORITE IN OUR MAIL-ORDER CATALOG. THE SECRET WAS TO TRANSFER FROM OUR DISPOSABLE CONTAINER INTO YOUR CASSEROLE DISH AND SAY YOU MADE IT!

BITSY'S MEATLOAF

My sister Bitsy gave me her meatloaf recipe years ago, and it's become a family favorite. On The VeryVera Show, I'm known to add a twist to traditional recipes, so I've changed the ketchup to marinara sauce in this recipe to add a punch of flavor. Adding more sauce during the baking time will help the meatloaf stay moist. I hope this will be your family's new go-to meatloaf recipe!

SERVES: 4 TO 6 | **PREP TIME: 30 MINUTES** | **COOK TIME: 50 TO 55 MINUTES**

MEATLOAF

1½ pounds ground beef (80/20 ground chuck recommended)

¼ pound hot pork sausage (Jimmy Dean® recommended)

1 cup panko bread crumbs

1 large egg

1½ teaspoons salt

¼ teaspoon ground black pepper

1 medium Vidalia onion, chopped

½ cup marinara sauce

1 tablespoon Worcestershire sauce

SAUCE

½ cup marinara sauce

2 tablespoons yellow mustard

2 tablespoons dark brown sugar

2 tablespoons white vinegar

1. Preheat the oven to 350°F.

2. In a large bowl, mix all the meatloaf ingredients together until well incorporated.

3. In a separate bowl, mix together the sauce ingredients and set aside.

4. Press the meatloaf mixture into an 8 x 4-inch loaf pan.

5. Place in the oven and bake for 45 minutes.

6. Drain the fat and cover with the sauce.

7. Place back in the oven and bake for an additional 5 to 10 minutes.

8. Remove from the oven and let it rest for 10 minutes before slicing.

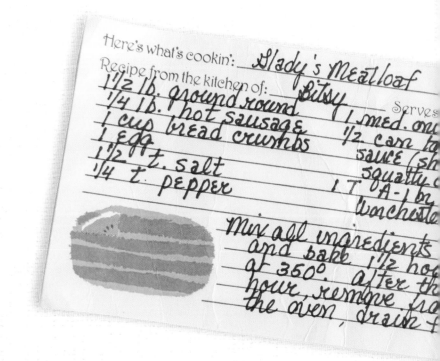

four cheese quiche

Quiche is classic for breakfast, lunch, or brunch. At the VeryVera Café, the topping for Four Cheese Quiche rotated daily. My personal favorites were the sautéed mushrooms and spinach or roasted asparagus tops. You can also opt to add another protein, like bacon or ham. Allow this basic recipe to be your canvas for creativity.

SERVES: 8 TO 10 | PREP TIME: 30 MINUTES | COOK TIME: 50 MINUTES

1 PILLSBURY® REFRIGERATED PIE CRUST

½ CUP SWISS CHEESE, HAND-SHREDDED

½ CUP CHEDDAR CHEESE, HAND-SHREDDED

½ CUP MOZZARELLA CHEESE, HAND-SHREDDED

5 LARGE EGGS

½ CUP RICOTTA CHEESE

1 CUP HEAVY CREAM

SALT, TO TASTE

GROUND BLACK PEPPER, TO TASTE

1. Preheat the oven to 350°F.

2. Line a 9-inch deep-dish pie pan with 1 pie crust.

3. Prick the pie shell, crimp the edges, and prebake at 350°F for 10 minutes.

4. Sprinkle the Swiss, cheddar, and mozzarella cheeses on the bottom of the prebaked pie shell.

5. In a large bowl, whisk together the eggs, ricotta, heavy cream, salt, and pepper.

6. Fill the pie shell with the egg mixture up to the edge of the crust.

7. Bake the quiche for 15 minutes.

8. Turn the oven down to 275°F.

9. Resume baking the quiche for another 25 minutes.

10. The quiche is done when it is set in the center. If it jiggles or appears loose, continue baking until a knife inserted in the middle comes out clean. It will puff up considerably while hot, but will fall once it has cooled. Let cool for 10 minutes before serving.

11. Refrigerate any leftover quiche. To reheat, slice the cold quiche into an individual serving and place on a microwavable plate. Microwave in 30-second intervals for up to $1\frac{1}{2}$ minutes or until hot throughout.

NOTE: MY MAMA ALWAYS PUT HAND-SHREDDED SHARP CHEDDAR CHEESE ON WARM APPLE PIE. WARM APPLE PIE FILLING ON TOP OF THIS QUICHE IS FABULOUS FOR A BRUNCH.

chicken poppy seed casserole

A potluck favorite for years, Chicken Poppy Seed Casserole is a creamy dish that satisfies during any season. This variation includes egg noodles, which add texture and allow this recipe to serve more people. Crushed Ritz® crackers create a savory and crunchy topping for this Southern classic. Here's a tip: crush the crackers while they are still in the sleeve to save on mess.

SERVES: 6 TO 8 | PREP TIME: 40 TO 45 MINUTES | BAKE TIME: 30 TO 40 MINUTES

CASSEROLE

½ POUND EGG NOODLES

1 STICK UNSALTED BUTTER

½ CUP ONIONS, DICED

1 (4-OUNCE) CAN SLICED MUSHROOMS, DRAINED

¾ TEASPOON CHICKEN BASE

1 CAN CREAM OF CHICKEN SOUP

4 BONELESS, SKINLESS CHICKEN BREASTS, COOKED AND SHREDDED (ABOUT 1½ POUNDS CHICKEN)

1 CUP SOUR CREAM

SALT, TO TASTE

GROUND BLACK PEPPER, TO TASTE

TOPPING

2 LARGE SLEEVES RITZ CRACKERS, CRUSHED

½ STICK SALTED BUTTER, MELTED

2 TABLESPOONS POPPY SEEDS

1. Preheat the oven to 325°F and grease a 7 x 11-inch pan with cooking spray.

2. Cook the egg noodles according to the package directions and set aside.

3. Melt the butter for the casserole in a large sauté pan over medium-high heat.

4. Sauté the onions and mushrooms until the onions are translucent.

5. Add the chicken base and mix well.

6. Stir in the cream of chicken soup, shredded chicken, and sour cream.

7. In a large bowl, mix together the egg noodles and the chicken mixture until well blended.

8. Mix together the crushed Ritz crackers, butter, and poppy seeds.

9. Pour half of the cracker mixture in the bottom of the pan, pour the casserole mixture in the pan, and top with the remaining cracker mixture.

10. Place in the oven and bake for 30 to 40 minutes or until hot and bubbling.

NOTE: THIS IS A GREAT CASSEROLE TO MAKE AHEAD OF TIME AND FREEZE. IF YOU ARE GOING TO FREEZE IT, STOP AFTER STEP 9. WHEN YOU DECIDE TO BAKE IT, FOR BEST RESULTS, THAW THE CASSEROLE OVERNIGHT IN THE FRIDGE, THEN PROCEED WITH BAKING.

layer CAKES

$\mathcal{M}$y first introduction to a layer cake was in the form of a birthday cake. Everyone in my family had the privilege of choosing their favorite to have on their birthday. It never occurred to me until now that my Mama knew how to bake all those different sorts of cakes, all in that tiny kitchen with five children running around.

Layer cakes are much easier to mix up than pound cakes and take a lot less time to bake. VeryVera layer cakes typically have 3 layers, freeze beautifully, stay fresh for a week, and are best served at room temperature.

CONVENTION VS. CONVECTION

Conventional ovens are more universal, but I prefer some baking in a convection oven, especially if you're baking in multiple pans. Even so, all ovens bake differently, and this is why we suggest a range for baking time. Be sure to keep an eye on the cakes, and if you start to smell them, check them. I also set my timer about 10 minutes early when preparing a recipe for the first time. The best way to check the doneness of the cake will be to touch the top gently. If there is no indentation, or if it immediately springs back, the cake is done. If an indentation stays in the cake, then you will need to bake the cake for 2 to 3 minutes longer.

PANS

Always be sure to use properly sized pans. Measure from inside edge to inside edge. For the layer cakes in this book, use a 9-inch pan. The batter should fill the pans halfway up. Using an incorrect pan size will result in a different cooking time. Before you preheat your oven, do a test to make sure all three pans will fit with at least a 1-inch border between each pan. If the pans don't fit, place two on the middle rack and one on the lower rack. Rotate the pans halfway through the cooking process. To prepare your pans for the layer cakes, line the pans with parchment paper and spray with floured baking spray.

choosing your ingredients

FLOUR

At VeryVera, we were known for our light and fluffy cakes. To ensure the right texture of the cake, use cake flour. Cake flour has less protein than all-purpose flour. Less protein means less gluten, which will create a lighter and fluffier cake. Too much gluten can make a cake tough and rubbery. Cake flour is also pre-sifted, which helps create the correct cake texture. If you do not have cake flour, all-purpose flour can be substituted with this simple trick: measure 1 cup of all-purpose flour, then remove 2 tablespoons. Add in 2 tablespoons of corn starch and sift the mixture at least 5 times. Although I do suggest using real cake flour, this method can be used in a bind.

BUTTER, MILK, AND EGGS

All the baked goods in this book will use unsalted butter, whole milk or heavy cream, and large or extra-large eggs. Use unsalted butter so you can control the amount of salt in the recipe. If you do use salted butter, cut down the other added salt by half. You always want your butter and eggs to be room temperature. Cold ingredients won't trap and hold air bubbles, which is what helps a cake rise. Let the butter sit at room temperature for at least an hour before beginning. To quickly warm cold eggs, place the whole eggs in a bowl of hot tap water for 10 minutes. Be careful not to leave the eggs in for too long, as they may begin to cook in the hot water.

CHOCOLATE LAYER (PAGE 114); STRAWBERRY LAYER (PAGE 107) ; YELLOW LAYER (PAGE 117); ICING (PAGE 100).

ICING

I know that technically most of my icings are frostings per the definition. However, when the word "frosting" comes to mind it makes the cake snob come out, and I think of shortening. "Icing" evokes elegance, time, and "boutique." VeryVera says icing, not frosting. All cream cheese icings should be stored in the refrigerator until use. When ready to begin icing a cake, the icing will need to come to room temperature to be spreadable. If possible, the cooked icings should be made and used immediately. If you are not able to do this, warm small amounts of the icing in the microwave until the consistency is smooth and easy to spread.

CHOCOLATE CAKE

Just like every lady needs a basic black dress, everyone needs a go-to chocolate cake. Starting with the basic yellow layers, we like to dress it up with a cooked chocolate icing similar to fudge. Need another accessory? We recommend adding some whipped cream on the side. For many of our traditional cake lovers, this was considered the ultimate birthday cake.

SERVES: 20 TO 24 (¾" OR 1" SLICES) | PREP TIME: 30 TO 45 MINUTES | BAKE TIME: 18 TO 20 MINUTES

Floured baking spray

1⅓ cups unsalted butter, at room temperature

2⅔ cups granulated sugar

5 extra-large eggs, at room temperature

4 cups cake flour

4 teaspoons baking powder

¾ teaspoon salt

2 cups whole milk, at room temperature

1⅓ teaspoons pure vanilla extract

ICING

1 cup unsalted butter

1 cup Hershey's® cocoa powder, sifted

8 cups confectioners' sugar, sifted

⅔ cup whole milk

1½ tablespoons pure vanilla extract

1. Preheat the oven to 400°F. Grease and flour three 9-inch pans lined with parchment paper.

2. Cream the butter and sugar in the bowl of a stand mixer on medium speed for 5 minutes, or until light and fluffy.

3. Add the eggs one at a time, beating well after each addition.

4. Scrape the sides and bottom of the bowl.

5. Combine the cake flour, baking powder, and salt in a bowl and mix with a wire whisk.

6. Combine the milk and vanilla extract in a liquid measuring cup.

7. With the mixer on low, alternately add the flour mixture and the milk mixture, beginning and ending with the flour mixture, beating until well blended.

8. Scrape the sides of the bowl and incorporate any unmixed batter if necessary.

9. Beat the batter for 7 minutes on medium speed.

10. Divide the batter evenly between the three prepared pans. Tap the pans on the counter to ensure there are no air bubbles.

11. Bake for 18 to 20 minutes. Test doneness by touching a cake top. If it springs back, it is done. If the indentation stays, it needs 2 to 3 minutes longer.

12. Cool the cakes for at least 10 minutes on a cooling rack before removing from the pans.

ICING

1. Melt the butter in a medium saucepan over medium heat.

2. Add the cocoa powder and whisk until all the lumps are dissolved.

3. Add ¼ of the confectioners' sugar and then add ¼ of the milk. Alternate until all the sugar and milk are incorporated.

4. Remove from the heat.

5. Add the vanilla extract and mix until well blended.

6. While the icing is still warm, frost the cooled cake layers: Spread icing between the cake layers and then on the top and sides of the stacked layers. The icing will set up like fudge as it cools.

7. If the mixture hardens while frosting the cake, warm the icing in the microwave at 10-second intervals until the smooth, velvety texture has returned.

Our magnets started as a simple marketing tool attached to each can with a few notes about our cakes' shelf life. Eventually, they became part of every household that ordered from VeryVera. I remember my son John calling from a ski lodge in Colorado to say "Mom, there's a VeryVera magnet on the fridge."

hummingbird cake

The Hummingbird Cake is one of the quintessential Southern layer cakes. Popularized by Southern Living when the magazine published a recipe by Mrs. L. H. Wiggins, it is the perfect autumn cake. I have to laugh when thinking about this dessert ... the cake named after a tiny bird is one of our tallest!

SERVES: 20 TO 24 (¾" OR 1" SLICES) | MAKES A 9-INCH, 4-LAYER CAKE | PREP TIME: 30 TO 45 MINUTES | BAKE TIME: 35 TO 40 MINUTES

FLOURED BAKING SPRAY

3 CUPS GRANULATED SUGAR

2¼ CUPS WESSON® VEGETABLE OIL

3 RIPE BANANAS, CHOPPED

5 LARGE EGGS, AT ROOM TEMPERATURE

2¼ TEASPOONS PURE VANILLA EXTRACT

4½ CUPS CAKE FLOUR

1½ TEASPOONS BAKING SODA

1½ TEASPOONS SALT

1½ TEASPOONS CINNAMON

12 OUNCES CRUSHED PINEAPPLE, DRAINED

¾ CUP PECANS, CHOPPED

ICING

1 STICK UNSALTED BUTTER, AT ROOM TEMPERATURE

16 OUNCES CREAM CHEESE, AT ROOM TEMPERATURE

1 TABLESPOON PURE VANILLA EXTRACT

2 POUNDS CONFECTIONERS' SUGAR

1. Preheat the oven to 325°F. Grease and flour four 9-inch pans lined with parchment paper.

2. Beat the sugar, oil, and bananas in the bowl of a stand mixer on low speed until bananas are broken down, about 3 minutes.

3. Scrape the sides and bottom of the bowl.

4. Add the eggs one at a time, beating well after each addition.

5. Add the vanilla and beat well.

6. Combine the cake flour, baking soda, salt, and cinnamon in a bowl and mix with a wire whisk.

7. With the mixer on low, add the flour mixture slowly and beat until well blended.

8. Scrape the sides of the bowl and incorporate any unmixed batter if necessary.

9. Beat the batter for 7 minutes on medium speed.

10. Add the crushed pineapple and chopped pecans to the batter and mix until well blended.

11. Divide the batter evenly between the four prepared pans. Tap the pans on the counter to ensure there are no air bubbles.

12. Bake for 35 to 40 minutes. Test doneness by touching a cake top. If it springs back, it is done. If the indentation stays, it needs 2 to 3 minutes longer.

13. Cool the cakes for at least 10 minutes on a cooling rack before removing from the pans.

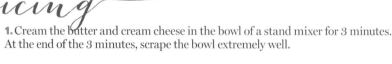

icing

1. Cream the butter and cream cheese in the bowl of a stand mixer for 3 minutes. At the end of the 3 minutes, scrape the bowl extremely well.

2. Add the vanilla extract and beat for 1 to 2 minutes.

3. Slowly add the confectioners' sugar, beating on low to ensure the sugar does not fly out of the mixing bowl.

4. After each addition of confectioners' sugar, scrape the bowl extremely well.

5. Once all the confectioners' sugar is incorporated, beat on low speed for 3 minutes.

6. Spread icing between the cake layers and then on the top and sides of the stacked layers.

RED VELVET CAKE

Christmas in the South wouldn't be the same without Red Velvet Cake. You could describe it as a slight vanilla flavor combined with a hint of chocolate. I'll never forget a lady calling VeryVera from San Francisco and asking for me. All she wanted to say was, "How in the world is this transplanted Southerner sitting on her porch in San Francisco eating a Red Velvet Cake that looks like it just left your bakery?" It's magic!

SERVES: 20 TO 24 (¾" OR 1" SLICES) | PREP TIME: 30 TO 45 MINUTES | BAKE TIME: 28 TO 30 MINUTES

Floured baking spray

1½ cups Wesson® vegetable oil

3 cups granulated sugar

1½ ounces red food coloring

5 large eggs, at room temperature

4½ cups cake flour

4½ tablespoons Hershey's® cocoa powder

1½ teaspoons baking soda

¾ teaspoon salt

1½ cups buttermilk, at room temperature

1½ teaspoons pure vanilla extract

1½ teaspoon white distilled vinegar

1 recipe Cream Cheese Icing (page 100)

1. Preheat the oven to 325°F. Grease and flour three 9-inch pans lined with parchment paper.

2. Beat the oil, sugar, and red food coloring in the bowl of a stand mixer on low speed for 5 minutes.

3. Scrape the sides and bottom of the bowl.

4. Add the eggs one at a time, beating well after each addition

5. Combine the dry ingredients in a separate bowl and stir with a wire whisk to mix.

6. Combine the buttermilk, vanilla, and vinegar in a large liquid measuring cup.

7. Alternately add the dry ingredients and the buttermilk mixture to the mixing bowl, starting and ending with the dry ingredients, beating until well blended.

8. Scrape the sides of the bowl and incorporate any unmixed batter if necessary.

9. Divide the batter evenly between the three prepared pans. Tap the pans on the counter to ensure there are no air bubbles.

10. Bake for 28 to 30 minutes. Test doneness by touching a cake top. If it springs back, it is done. If the indentation stays, it needs 2 to 3 minutes longer.

11. Cool the cakes for at least 10 minutes on a cooling rack before removing from the pans.

12. Prepare the cream cheese icing and ice the cooled layers.

NOT JUST RED VELVET – BUT DESIGNER STYLE

Sending cakes to magazines was a summer ritual at VeryVera. We would make a list, research the right editor to receive the gift, try to nail down whether that person would be in the office on a particular day, and then present a cake and an editorial idea that would WOW the recipient. My best example is the year we sent Red Velvet. We made a swatch sample of red velvet fabric attached to cardboard hangers complete with fabric instructions, just like you would see in a decorator's warehouse. We then created a gift enclosure that read, "We think FABRIC makes a wonderful gift." Upon opening the card, it read, "We recommend Red Velvet." Under the card was our signature Red Velvet Cake for the editor to enjoy. The editor at Town & Country thought the whole idea was smashing, and when their December issue had no room for another article, he asked if he could put a Valentine's Day spin on the idea. Why not?! We made the February issue.

FEATURED IN

NY Times Best of the Season, Veranda, Better Homes and Gardens, Town & Country, Parade Magazine, Cottage Living, Southern Living, Saks.com

german chocolate cake

This cake seems too sophisticated for a little girl's birthday, but it has always been my absolute favorite, even today. I was never a fan of a store-bought cake, and I loved the chunkiness and richness of this one. It will impress your guests.

SERVES: 20 TO 24 (¾" OR 1" SLICES) | PREP TIME: 30 TO 45 MINUTES | BAKE TIME: 30 MINUTES

FLOURED BAKING SPRAY

½ CUP WATER

4 OUNCES BAKER'S® GERMAN'S SWEET CHOCOLATE

1 CUP UNSALTED BUTTER, AT ROOM TEMPERATURE

2 CUPS GRANULATED SUGAR

4 LARGE EGGS, AT ROOM TEMPERATURE

3 CUPS CAKE FLOUR

1 TEASPOON BAKING SODA

½ TEASPOON SALT

1 CUP BUTTERMILK, AT ROOM TEMPERATURE

1 TEASPOON PURE VANILLA EXTRACT

ICING

2 ⅔ CUPS SWEETENED COCONUT FLAKES

2 CUPS PECANS, CHOPPED

1 CUP UNSALTED BUTTER

2 CUPS EVAPORATED MILK

2 CUPS GRANULATED SUGAR

8 LARGE EGG YOLKS

2 TEASPOONS PURE VANILLA EXTRACT

1. Preheat the oven to 325°F. Grease and flour three 9-inch pans lined with parchment paper.

2. Heat the water and chocolate together in a microwave for about 1 minute. Stir the mixture. Place in the microwave again if needed to melt the chocolate. Allow the chocolate to cool before adding it to the other ingredients.

3. Cream the butter and sugar in the bowl of a stand mixer on medium speed for 5 minutes, or until light and fluffy.

4. Add the eggs one at a time, beating well after each addition.

5. Scrape the sides and bottom of the bowl very well.

6. Add the chocolate mixture and combine.

7. Combine the cake flour, baking soda, and salt in a bowl and mix with a wire whisk.

8. Combine the buttermilk and vanilla in a liquid measuring cup.

9. Alternately add the flour mixture and the buttermilk mixture, beginning and ending with the flour mixture, beating until well blended.

10. Scrape the sides and bottom of the bowl and incorporate any unmixed batter if necessary.

11. Beat the batter for 3 minutes on medium speed.

12. Divide the batter evenly between the three prepared pans. Tap the pans on the counter to ensure there are no air bubbles.

13. Bake for 30 minutes. Test doneness by touching a cake top. If it springs back, it is done. If the indentation stays, it needs 2 to 3 minutes longer.

14. Cool the cakes for at least 10 minutes on a cooling rack before removing from the pans.

icing

1. Place the coconut and pecans in a bowl together and set aside.

2. In a medium saucepan, melt the butter over medium heat.

3. Add the evaporated milk and sugar and bring to a boil.

4. Slowly add half of the milk mixture to the egg yolks, whisking vigorously until combined.

5. Place the egg mixture back in the saucepan and stir constantly over medium heat for about 3 to 4 minutes, until you see a bubble and the mixture has thickened.

6. Pour the egg and milk mixture over the pecans and coconut.

7. Add the vanilla and stir until well blended.

8. Let the icing cool.

9. Once the icing is cool, spread it between the cake layers, sides, and on top.

STRAWBERRY CAKE

This 1940s vintage recipe, which I truly thought my grandmother made up, has turned up in many "grandmother-inspired" cookbooks. Our version won the hearts of our customers through its association with my annual gift to the American Cancer Society in memory of my mother. It became famous when Oprah picked it as her favorite in the April 2009 issue of O, The Oprah Magazine.

SERVES: 20 TO 24 (¾" OR 1" SLICES) | PREP TIME: 30 TO 45 MINUTES | BAKE TIME: 28 TO 30 MINUTES

Floured baking spray

1 (8-ounce) package frozen sliced strawberries with sugar added, thawed

4 cups Betty Crocker® white cake mix*

3 ounces strawberry Jell-O® mix

4 large eggs, at room temperature

½ cup vegetable oil

½ cup whole milk, at room temperature

⅓ cup all-purpose flour

ICING

1 stick unsalted butter, at room temperature

16 ounces cream cheese, at room temperature

½ teaspoon strawberry extract

2 pounds confectioners' sugar

6 drops red food coloring

*This will require 2 boxes of cake mix to be purchased.

1. Preheat the oven to 325°F. Grease and flour three 9-inch pans lined with parchment paper.

2. Place the thawed strawberries in a food processor and pulse to puree. Measure ½ cup to use for this recipe and freeze the rest for the next time you make this cake.

3. Combine the cake mix and the Jell-O mix with a spatula.

4. Add the ½ cup of strawberry puree, eggs, and oil and mix until well blended.

5. Add the milk to the Jell-O mixture and beat vigorously for 2 minutes.

6. Add the flour and mix, just until the batter is smooth.

7. Divide the batter evenly between the three prepared pans. Tap the pans on the counter to ensure there are no air bubbles.

8. Bake for 28 to 30 minutes. Test doneness by touching a cake top. If it springs back, it is done. If the indentation stays, it needs 2 to 3 minutes longer. If needed, use a wooden skewer.

9. Cool the cakes for at least 10 minutes on a cooling rack before removing from the pans.

A Team Effort to Fight Cancer

In a tribute to Mothers everywhere, Very Vera introduces an anual gift that will benefit The American Cancer Society. In honor of Vera's mother, Betty Wingfield, $2.00 from every sale of the Strawberry Layer cake will be donated to help find a cure for the disease that takes the lives of so many each year.

AMERICAN CANCER SOCIETY

ICING

1. Cream the butter and cream cheese in the bowl of a stand mixer for 3 minutes. At the end of the 3 minutes, scrape the bowl extremely well.

2. Add the strawberry extract and beat for 1 to 2 minutes.

3. Slowly add the confectioners' sugar, beating on low to ensure the sugar does not fly out of the mixing bowl.

4. After each addition of confectioners' sugar, scrape the bottom of the bowl extremely well.

5. Once all the confectioners' sugar is incorporated, add the red food coloring and beat on low for 3 minutes.

6. Spread icing between the cake layers and then on the top and sides of the stacked layers.

CONTINUED ON 108

THIS IS ONE OF OUR ORIGINAL SERVING KNIVES FROM VERYVERA IN 1994.

CONTINUED FROM 107

STRAWBERRY SHORT LIST

I always had a bug in my bonnet, and for years it was getting one of my cakes in front of Oprah. I began sending them to her with a note and would always get a nice reply in the mail as a thank-you for sending it, along with glowing reviews of the cake. After a couple of years of doing this, Oprah's friend Gayle King started ordering from us and would not only order cakes, but the entire Thanksgiving meal for her family. This continued for several years, as did my traditional cake teaser delivery, as I hoped for an opportunity to be chosen for Oprah's O List. Persistence pays off, and after 10 years of cakes, we got the call that our Strawberry Layer Cake made the list. It was worth the wait, as the issue we were featured in was also historic for O Magazine: It was the first time Oprah shared the cover, with Michelle Obama. We had record sales for Mother's Day that year.

FEATURED IN — *Cooking with Paula Deen, O, The Oprah Magazine, Chrysler Magazine, Reno Magazine, InStyle, USA Weekend, American Homestyle and Gardening*

SNACKING IN STYLE

We trimmed the tops off of the cakes (page 123) and those would go to waste or get consumed by our staff. If we loved the scraps that much, we thought our customers would, too. The scraps got packaged in sandwich bags and were placed in a basket as a "favor" when you left.

LEMON CAKE

Few flavors scream summer quite like lemon. Transform a traditional yellow cake and cream cheese icing with lemon and you have VeryVera's Lemon Cake, which was our April Cake of the Month. This sweet and tart cake is the perfect accompaniment to your summer spread or a great ending to a heavy meal.

SERVES: 20 TO 24 (¾" OR 1" SLICES) | PREP TIME: 30 TO 45 MINUTES | BAKE TIME: 18 TO 20 MINUTES

Floured baking spray

1⅓ cups unsalted butter, at room temperature

2⅔ cups granulated sugar

5 extra-large eggs, at room temperature

4 cups cake flour

4 teaspoons baking powder

¾ teaspoon salt

2 cups whole milk, at room temperature

½ teaspoon pure vanilla extract

1⅓ teaspoons lemon extract

Zest of 1 lemon

ICING

1 stick unsalted butter, at room temperature

16 ounces cream cheese, at room temperature

1 teaspoon pure vanilla extract

2 teaspoons lemon extract

2 pounds confectioners' sugar

Zest of ½ lemon

1. Preheat the oven to 400°F. Grease and flour three 9-inch pans lined with parchment paper.

2. Cream the butter and sugar in the bowl of a stand mixer on medium speed for 5 minutes, or until light and fluffy.

3. Scrape the sides and bottom of the bowl.

4. Add the eggs one at a time, beating well after each addition.

5. Scrape the sides and bottom of the bowl again.

6. Combine the cake flour, baking powder, and salt in a bowl and mix with a wire whisk.

7. Combine the milk, vanilla extract, and lemon extract in a liquid measuring cup.

8. With the mixer on low, alternately add the flour mixture and the milk mixture, beginning with the flour mixture and ending with the milk mixture, beating until well blended.

9. Beat the batter for 7 minutes on low speed.

10. Add the lemon zest and beat until incorporated.

11. Divide the batter evenly between the three prepared pans. Tap the pans on the counter to ensure there are no air bubbles.

12. Bake for 18 to 20 minutes. Test doneness by touching the top. If it springs back, it is done. If the indentation stays, it needs 2 to 3 minutes longer.

13. Cool the cakes for at least 10 minutes on a cooling rack before removing from pans.

ICING

1. Cream the butter and cream cheese in the bowl of a stand mixer for 3 minutes. At the end of the 3 minutes, scrape the bowl extremely well.

2. Add the vanilla and lemon extracts and beat for 1 to 2 minutes.

3. Slowly add the confectioners' sugar, beating on low to ensure the sugar does not fly out of the mixing bowl.

4. After each addition of confectioners' sugar, scrape the bottom of the bowl extremely well.

5. Add the lemon zest and beat on low for 3 minutes.

6. Spread icing between the cake layers and then on the top and sides of the stacked layers.

BAILEYS IRISH CREAM CAKE

With a hint of Baileys Irish Cream, this moist cake was our March Cake of the Month. The Irish cream flavor is subtle, so I like to add some extra rum and butter flavoring, which enhances the flavor of the layers. Our regular Cake of the Month customers couldn't wait for this cake, and instead of waiting for Saint Patrick's Day, theirs shipped on March 1st. This cake is perfect with a cup of coffee.

SERVES: 20 TO 24 (¾" OR 1" SLICES) | PREP TIME: 30 TO 45 MINUTES | BAKE TIME: 18 TO 20 MINUTES

Floured baking spray

1⅓ cups unsalted butter, at room temperature

2⅔ cups granulated sugar

5 extra-large eggs, at room temperature

4 cups cake flour

4 teaspoons baking powder

¾ teaspoon salt

1⅓ cups whole milk, at room temperature

½ teaspoon pure vanilla extract

½ teaspoon rum flavoring

½ teaspoon butter flavoring

⅔ cup Baileys Irish Cream

ICING

1 stick unsalted butter, at room temperature

16 ounces cream cheese, at room temperature

1 teaspoon pure vanilla extract

2 teaspoons Baileys Irish Cream

2 pounds confectioners' sugar

1. Preheat the oven to 400°F. Grease and flour three 9-inch pans lined with parchment paper.

2. Cream the butter and sugar in the bowl of a stand mixer on medium speed for 5 minutes, or until light and fluffy.

3. Scrape the sides and bottom of the bowl.

4. Add the eggs one at a time, beating well after each addition.

5. Combine the cake flour, baking powder, and salt in a bowl and mix with a wire whisk.

6. Combine the milk, flavorings, and Baileys Irish Cream in a large liquid measuring cup.

7. With the mixer on low, alternately add the flour mixture and the milk mixture, beginning and ending with the flour mixture, beating until well blended.

8. Scrape the sides of the bowl and incorporate any unmixed batter if necessary.

9. Beat the batter for 7 minutes on medium speed.

10. Divide the batter evenly between the three prepared pans. Tap the pans on the counter to ensure there are no air bubbles.

11. Bake for 18 to 20 minutes. Test doneness by touching a cake top. If it springs back, it is done. If the indentation stays, it needs 2 to 3 minutes longer.

12. Cool the cakes for at least 10 minutes on a cooling rack before removing from the pans.

ICING

1. Cream the butter and cream cheese in the bowl of a stand mixer for 3 minutes. At the end of the 3 minutes, scrape the bowl extremely well.

2. Add the vanilla extract and Baileys Irish Cream and beat for 1 to 2 minutes.

3. Slowly add the confectioners' sugar, beating on low to ensure the sugar does not fly out of the mixing bowl.

4. After each addition of confectioners' sugar, scrape the bottom and sides of the bowl extremely well.

5. Once all the confectioners' sugar is incorporated, beat on low for 3 minutes.

6. Spread icing between the cake layers and then on the top and sides of the stacked layers.

chocolate-covered strawberry cake

As the February Cake of the Month at VeryVera, this is the perfect cake to make for your sweetheart. This year, instead of sticking to chocolate-covered strawberries, change it up in cake form.

SERVES: 20 TO 24 (¾" OR 1" SLICES) | PREP TIME: 30 TO 45 MINUTES | BAKE TIME: 28 TO 30 MINUTES

FLOURED BAKING SPRAY

1 (8-OUNCE) PACKAGE FROZEN SLICED STRAWBERRIES WITH SUGAR ADDED, THAWED

4 CUPS BETTY CROCKER® WHITE CAKE MIX*

3 OUNCES STRAWBERRY JELL-O® MIX

4 LARGE EGGS

½ CUP VEGETABLE OIL

½ CUP WHOLE MILK, AT ROOM TEMPERATURE

⅓ CUP ALL-PURPOSE FLOUR

ICING

1 CUP UNSALTED BUTTER

1 CUP HERSHEY'S® COCOA POWDER, SIFTED

8 CUPS CONFECTIONERS' SUGAR, SIFTED

⅔ CUP WHOLE MILK

1½ TABLESPOONS PURE VANILLA EXTRACT

*THIS WILL REQUIRE 2 BOXES OF CAKE MIX TO BE PURCHASED.

1. Preheat the oven to 325°F. Grease and flour three 9-inch pans lined with parchment paper.

2. Place the thawed strawberries in a food processor and pulse to puree. Measure $\frac{1}{2}$ cup to use for this recipe and freeze the rest for the next time you make this cake.

3. Combine the cake mix and Jell-O mix with a rubber spatula.

4. Add the $\frac{1}{2}$ cup of strawberry puree, eggs, and oil and mix until well blended.

5. Add the milk to Jell-O mixture and beat vigorously for 2 minutes.

6. Add the flour and mix, just until the batter is smooth.

7. Divide the batter evenly between the three prepared pans. Tap the pans on the counter to ensure there are no air bubbles.

8. Bake for 28 to 30 minutes. Test doneness by touching a cake top. If it springs back, it is done. If the indentation stays, it needs 2 to 3 minutes longer. If needed, use a wooden skewer.

9. Cool the cakes for at least 10 minutes on a cooling rack before removing from the pans.

icing

1. Melt the butter in a medium saucepan over medium heat.

2. Add the cocoa powder and whisk until all the lumps are dissolved.

3. Add $\frac{1}{4}$ of the confectioners' sugar and then $\frac{1}{4}$ of the milk. Alternate until all the sugar and milk are incorporated.

4. Remove from the heat.

5. Add the vanilla extract and mix until well blended.

6. While the icing is still warm, frost the cooled cake layers: Spread icing between the cake layers and then on the top and sides of the stacked layers. The icing will set up like fudge as it cools.

7. If the mixture hardens while frosting the cake, warm the icing in the microwave in 10-second intervals until the smooth, velvety texture has returned.

devil's food cake

A chocolate cake is the answer to most any occasion. Chocolate is my personal favorite sweet treat, and this cake is therefore scrumptious to me! My preference is to serve this cake at room temperature. This allows the taster to enjoy the cake and icing at their most velvety, when the chocolate flavor comes through in its purest form.

SERVES: 20 TO 24 (¾" OR 1" SLICES) | PREP TIME: 30 TO 45 MINUTES | BAKE TIME: 20 TO 30 MINUTES

FLOURED BAKING SPRAY

1 CUP UNSALTED BUTTER, AT ROOM TEMPERATURE

2 CUPS GRANULATED SUGAR

3 LARGE EGGS, AT ROOM TEMPERATURE

2 CUPS CAKE FLOUR

1 CUP HERSHEY'S® COCOA POWDER

2 TEASPOONS BAKING SODA

1 TEASPOON SALT

2 CUPS BUTTERMILK, AT ROOM TEMPERATURE

1 TABLESPOON PURE VANILLA EXTRACT

ICING

1 CUP UNSALTED BUTTER

1 CUP HERSHEY'S® COCOA POWDER, SIFTED

8 CUPS CONFECTIONERS' SUGAR, SIFTED

⅔ CUP WHOLE MILK

1½ TABLESPOONS PURE VANILLA EXTRACT

1. Preheat the oven to 300°F. Grease and flour three 9-inch pans lined with parchment paper.

2. Cream the butter and sugar in the bowl of a stand mixer on medium speed for 5 minutes, or until light and fluffy.

3. Scrape the sides and bottom of the bowl.

4. Add the eggs one at a time, beating well after each addition.

5. Scrape the sides and bottom of the bowl.

6. Combine the cake flour, cocoa, baking soda, and salt in a bowl and mix with a wire whisk.

7. Combine the buttermilk and vanilla extract in a liquid measuring cup.

8. With the mixer on low, alternately add the flour mixture and the buttermilk mixture, beginning and ending with the flour mixture, beating until well blended.

9. Scrape the sides of the bowl and incorporate any unmixed batter if necessary.

10. Divide the batter evenly between the three prepared pans. Tap the pans on the counter to ensure there are no air bubbles.

11. Bake for 20 to 30 minutes. Test doneness by touching a cake top. If it springs back, it is done. If the indentation stays, it needs 2 to 3 minutes longer.

12. Cool the cakes for at least 10 minutes on a cooling rack before removing from the pans.

icing

1. Melt the butter in a medium saucepan over medium heat.

2. Add the cocoa powder and whisk until all the lumps are dissolved.

3. Add $\frac{1}{4}$ of the confectioners' sugar and then $\frac{1}{4}$ of the milk. Alternate until all the sugar and milk are incorporated.

4. Remove from the heat.

5. Add the vanilla extract and mix until well blended.

6. While the icing is still warm, frost the cooled cake layers: Spread icing between the cake layers and then on the top and sides of the stacked layers. The icing will set up like fudge as it cools.

7. If the mixture hardens while icing, warm the icing in the microwave in 10-second intervals until the smooth, velvety texture has returned.

CARAMEL CAKE

Have you ever seen people get mad at a family reunion? Well, it only happened at ours if you had two people fighting over the last piece of my Aunt Libba's Caramel Cake! The dessert table took priority over fried chicken if her cake was on the buffet. This cake batter pours like pancake batter, and the result is a very moist cake.

SERVES: 20 TO 24 (¾" OR 1" SLICES) | **PREP TIME: 30 TO 45 MINUTES** | **BAKE TIME: 18 TO 20 MINUTES**

Floured baking spray

1⅓ cups unsalted butter, at room temperature

2⅔ cups granulated sugar

5 extra-large eggs, at room temperature

4 cups cake flour

4 teaspoons baking powder

¾ teaspoon salt

2 cups whole milk, at room temperature

1⅓ teaspoons pure vanilla extract

ICING

1 cup unsalted butter

1 pound Dixie Crystals® dark brown sugar

½ cup whole milk

3½ cups confectioners' sugar, sifted

1. Preheat the oven to 400°F. Grease and flour three 9-inch pans lined with parchment paper.

2. Cream the butter and sugar in the bowl of a stand mixer on medium speed for 5 minutes, or until light and fluffy.

3. Scrape the sides and bottom of the bowl.

4. Add the eggs one at a time, beating well after each addition.

5. Scrape the sides and bottom of the bowl again.

6. Combine the cake flour, baking powder, and salt in a bowl and mix with a wire whisk.

7. Combine the milk and vanilla extract in a liquid measuring cup.

8. With the mixer on low, alternately add the flour mixture and the milk mixture, beginning and ending with the flour mixture, beating until well blended.

9. Beat the batter for 7 minutes on medium speed.

10. Divide the batter evenly between the three prepared pans. Tap the pans on the counter to ensure there are no air bubbles.

11. Bake for 18 to 20 minutes. Test doneness by touching a cake top. If it springs back, it is done. If the indentation stays, it needs 2 to 3 minutes longer.

12. Cool the cakes for at least 10 minutes on a cooling rack before removing from the pans.

ICING

1. Melt the butter in a medium saucepan over medium heat.

2. Add the brown sugar and stir using a wire whisk until the butter is absorbed into the sugar. You will know the butter is absorbed because there will not be butter pieces floating on the top. Allow the mixture to bubble for about 2 minutes, stirring occasionally.

3. After 2 minutes, add the milk very carefully to the mixture to avoid splattering. Keep stirring and return the mixture to a full, rolling boil. Remove the mixture from the heat.

4. Add the mixture to the bowl of a stand mixer.

5. With the mixer on low speed and using the whisk attachment, gradually add the confectioners' sugar (1 cup at a time), mixing well after each addition of sugar. Mix until smooth and glossy; the icing should pour easily from the bowl.

6. While the icing is still warm, frost the cooled cake layers: Spread icing between the cake layers and then on the top and sides of the stacked layers. The icing will set up like candy as it cools.

7. If the mixture hardens while frosting the cake, warm the icing in the microwave in 10-second intervals until the smooth, velvety texture has returned.

FEATURED IN

InStyle Magazine, Veranda

CONTINUED ON 118

CONTINUED FROM 117

OSCAR DE LA RENTA'S VALENTINE SURPRISE

In 1997, John Rosselli & Associates was redecorating the Park Avenue address of Oscar de la Renta. Someone overheard him say his favorite dessert was Caramel Cake. John Rosselli's team knew just what to do and placed the order with VeryVera. To our surprise, a few days later we received a large order from Oscar sending Caramel Cakes to his Valentine's Day list. He endorsed our cake as his favorite thing in InStyle Magazine in 2006.

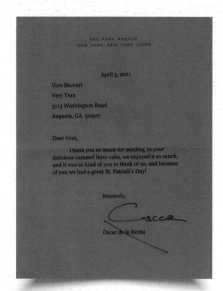

DOUBLE CHOCOLATE CAKE

How is it possible to make a chocolate cake even better? The answer: by adding another type of chocolate filling. Starting with layers of chocolate cake, this recipe adds a fudge-like cooked chocolate filling between the layers and finishes with a milk chocolate cream cheese icing on the outside. Enjoy with a glass of milk or a cup of coffee.

SERVES: 20 TO 24 (¾" OR 1" SLICES) | PREP TIME: 30 TO 45 MINUTES | BAKE TIME: 20 TO 30 MINUTES

Floured baking spray

1 cup unsalted butter, at room temperature

2 cups granulated sugar

3 large eggs, at room temperature

2 cups cake flour

1 cup Hershey's® cocoa powder

2 teaspoons baking soda

1 teaspoon salt

2 cups buttermilk, at room temperature

1 tablespoon pure vanilla extract

1. Preheat the oven to 300°F. Grease and flour three 9-inch pans lined with parchment paper.

2. Cream the butter and sugar in the bowl of a stand mixer on medium speed for 5 minutes, or until light and fluffy.

3. Scrape the sides and bottom of the bowl.

4. Add the eggs one at a time, beating well after each addition.

5. Scrape the sides and bottom of the bowl.

6. Combine the cake flour, cocoa, baking soda, and salt in a bowl and mix with a wire whisk.

7. Combine the buttermilk and vanilla extract in a liquid measuring cup.

8. With the mixer on low, alternately add the flour mixture and the buttermilk mixture, beginning and ending with the flour mixture, beating until well blended.

9. Scrape the sides of the bowl and incorporate any unmixed batter if necessary.

CHOCOLATE ICING (FILLING)

1 cup unsalted butter

1 cup Hershey's® cocoa powder, sifted

8 cups confectioners' sugar, sifted

²/₃ cup whole milk

1½ tablespoons pure vanilla extract

MILK CHOCOLATE ICING

1 stick unsalted butter, at room temperature

16 ounces cream cheese, at room temperature

1½ cups (9 ounces) milk chocolate

1 tablespoon pure vanilla extract

2 pounds (8 cups) confectioners' sugar

10. Divide the batter evenly between the three prepared pans. Tap the pans on the counter to ensure there are no air bubbles.

11. Bake for 20 to 30 minutes. Test doneness by touching a cake top. If it springs back, it is done. If the indentation stays, it needs 2 to 3 minutes longer.

12. Cool the cakes for at least 10 minutes on a cooling rack before removing from the pans.

FILLING

1. Melt the butter in a medium saucepan over medium heat.

2. Add the cocoa powder and whisk until all the lumps are dissolved.

3. Add ¼ of the confectioners' sugar and then ¼ of the milk. Alternate until all the sugar and milk are incorporated.

4. Remove from the heat.

5. Add the vanilla extract and mix until well blended.

6. While the filling is still warm, spread it between the cake layers. The filling will set up like fudge as it cools.

7. If the filling hardens while icing the layers, warm the filling in the microwave in 10-second intervals until the smooth, velvety texture has returned.

ICING

1. Cream the butter and cream cheese in the bowl of a stand mixer for 3 minutes. At the end of the 3 minutes, scrape the bowl extremely well.

2. Meanwhile, melt the chocolate in the microwave in 10-second intervals until smooth.

3. Add the melted chocolate to the butter and cream cheese with the mixer on low speed.

4. Add the vanilla and beat well.

5. Slowly add the confectioners' sugar, beating on low to ensure the sugar does not fly out of the mixing bowl.

6. After each addition of confectioners' sugar, scrape the bottom and sides of the bowl extremely well.

7. Once all the confectioners' sugar is incorporated, beat on low speed for 3 minutes.

8. Spread over the top and sides of the filled, stacked cake layers.

NOTE: CAKE LAYERS CAN BE MADE AHEAD AND FROZEN OR REFRIGERATED, TIGHTLY WRAPPED.

carrot cake

This is by far my most well-known cake. I am now often referred to as the "Carrot Cake Lady." The VeryVera Carrot Cake is the reigning champion that prevailed in battle against Food Network® star Bobby Flay. I still have blogs in which I was asked to surrender this recipe and I declined. Not until now has this secret been revealed.

SERVES: 20 TO 24 (¾" OR 1" SLICES) | PREP TIME: 30 TO 45 MINUTES | BAKE TIME: 30 MINUTES

FLOURED BAKING SPRAY

¾ CUP WESSON® VEGETABLE OIL

2 CUPS GRANULATED SUGAR

3 LARGE EGGS, AT ROOM TEMPERATURE

2 CUPS CAKE FLOUR

2 TEASPOONS BAKING SODA

1½ TEASPOONS SALT

1 TABLESPOON CINNAMON

⅛ TEASPOON GROUND NUTMEG

¾ CUP BUTTERMILK, AT ROOM TEMPERATURE

1 TEASPOON PURE VANILLA EXTRACT

2 CUPS HAND-SHREDDED CARROTS

8 OUNCES CRUSHED PINEAPPLE IN JUICE, DRAINED

1½ CUPS PECANS, CHOPPED

1 CUP SWEETENED COCONUT FLAKES

1 RECIPE CREAM CHEESE ICING (PAGE 100)

1. Preheat the oven to 325°F. Grease and flour three 9-inch pans lined with parchment paper.

2. Combine the oil and sugar in a large mixing bowl. Mix well with a rubber spatula.

3. Add the eggs one at a time, mixing until well blended.

4. Combine the dry ingredients in a separate bowl and mix with a wire whisk.

5. Combine the buttermilk and vanilla in a liquid measuring cup.

6. Alternately add the dry ingredients and the buttermilk mixture to the egg and oil mixture, beginning and ending with the dry ingredients.

7. Scrape the sides of the bowl and continue to mix.

8. Slowly add the carrots, drained pineapple, pecans, and coconut.

9. Divide the batter evenly between the three prepared pans. Tap the pans on the counter to ensure there are no air bubbles.

10. Bake for 30 minutes. Test doneness by touching a cake top. If it springs back, it is done. If the indentation stays, it needs 2 to 3 minutes longer.

11. Cool the cakes for at least 10 minutes on a cooling rack before removing from the pans.

12. Prepare the cream cheese icing and ice the cooled layers.

CARROT CAKE THROWDOWN

I'll never forget the call from the soon-to-be-launched Cooking Channel® in the winter of 2011. This scout was looking for guests for a new show called Top That Cake. She inquired if I would consider myself an expert on carrot cake. Of course, the answer was yes, and so we made plans for the crew to come to Augusta to film this show. It was such an exciting time getting VeryVera ready to be on TV and spending two glorious days being interviewed, filming, and inviting special customers to be part of the process. Day 2 was the big "finale" day. An audience of over 100 special guests was present to cheer me on as I gave enthusiastic instructions on baking the perfect carrot cake. A few minutes into the filming process, I noticed people staring, laughing, and pointing toward the front row. My whole life flashed before my eyes as I made eye contact with Bobby Flay! Not only was I now on the Food Network®, but I was being put to the ultimate test: a Throwdown to see which of us could make the best cake. I won the challenge but also walked away with one of the greatest experiences of my life. This cake shortly became one of my top three sellers, and I still get calls from would-be customers when this episode re-airs.

COCONUT CAKE

A Southern classic and our December Cake of the Month, the Coconut Cake uses both coconut extract and coconut milk. Instead of sprinkling the coconut on top, I like to mix it into the cream cheese icing. Keep this cake refrigerated and note that it may be good cold, but it's amazing at room temperature.

SERVES: 20 TO 24 (¾" OR 1" SLICES) | PREP TIME: 30 TO 45 MINUTES | BAKE TIME: 18 TO 20 MINUTES

Floured baking spray

1⅓ cups unsalted butter, at room temperature

2⅔ cups granulated sugar

5 extra-large eggs, at room temperature

4 cups cake flour

4 teaspoons baking powder

¾ teaspoon salt

1⅓ cups whole milk, at room temperature

½ teaspoon pure vanilla extract

1 teaspoon coconut extract

⅔ cup coconut milk

ICING

1 stick unsalted butter, at room temperature

16 ounces cream cheese, at room temperature

2 teaspoons coconut extract

1 teaspoon pure vanilla extract

2 pounds confectioners' sugar

2¼ cups sweetened coconut flakes

1. Preheat the oven to 400°F. Grease and flour three 9-inch pans lined with parchment paper.

2. Cream the butter and sugar in the bowl of a stand mixer on medium speed for 5 minutes, or until light and fluffy.

3. Scrape the sides and bottom of the bowl.

4. Add the eggs, one at a time, beating well after each addition.

5. Scrape the sides and bottom of the bowl again.

6. Combine the cake flour, baking powder, and salt in a bowl and mix with a wire whisk.

7. Combine the milk, flavorings, and coconut milk in a large liquid measuring cup.

8. With the mixer on low, alternately add the flour mixture and milk mixture, beginning and ending with flour mixture, beating until well blended.

9. Scrape the sides and bottom of the bowl and incorporate any unmixed batter if necessary.

10. Beat the batter for 7 minutes on medium speed.

11. Divide the batter evenly between the three prepared pans. Tap the pans on the counter to ensure there are no air bubbles.

12. Bake for 18 to 20 minutes. Test doneness by touching a cake top. If it springs back, it is done. If the indentation stays, it needs 2 to 3 minutes longer.

13. Cool the cakes for at least 10 minutes on a cooling rack before removing from the pans.

ICING

1. Cream the butter and cream cheese in the bowl of a stand mixer for 3 minutes. At the end of the 3 minutes, scrape the bowl extremely well.

2. Add the flavorings and beat for 1 to 2 minutes.

3. Slowly add the confectioners' sugar, beating on low to ensure the sugar does not fly out of the mixing bowl.

4. After each addition of confectioners' sugar, scrape the bottom of the bowl extremely well.

5. Once all the confectioners' sugar is incorporated, add the coconut and beat on low speed for 3 minutes.

6. Spread icing between the cake layers and then on the top and sides of the stacked layers.

FEATURED IN   *Veranda*

HOW TO ICE A VERYVERA LAYER CAKE

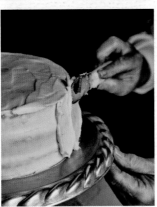

1.CRUMB COAT STEPS:

- Start with a cooled cake.

- If the cake has domed in the middle, you should cut off the domed part with a long, serrated knife. Use a baking sheet as a guide for the knife.

- Prepare a cake stand with a dollop of icing to hold the first layer in place. (You can also do this on a cardboard circle and transfer to a cake dome or pedestal.)

- Place the first layer down, bottom side up. Slide wax paper or parchment paper under the edges to keep the plate or cake stand clean.

- Put approximately 2/3 cup of icing in the center of the layer.

- Use an icing spatula to evenly distribute the icing all over the layer, going all the way to the edges.

- Do the same with the other layers.

- Spread a thin layer of icing on the sides and top of the cake to trap any loose crumbs and keep them from showing up in your final coat of icing.

- Put the cake in the freezer for 30 to 60 minutes to harden the crumb coat.

2. FINISHING COAT STEPS:

- Apply a coat of icing on the sides and top of the cake using an icing spatula.

- For the classic VeryVera cake look, do the "Kitty Swag & Swirl": For the swag, load a 5-inch metal spatula with a heaping amount of icing on the end. Press this against the cake and do a side-sweep motion to create a "swag" effect. Make sure you have enough icing to cover the appearance of layers. For the Swirl, start in the center of the cake with a loaded icing spatula. Sweep the spatula to about half an inch from the edge to create a 1-inch "petal." Continue around the cake for a flower design.

DON'T GIVE UP IF IT DOESN'T LOOK PERFECT THE FIRST TIME!

CHAPTER 6

sweet
TREATS

ime for dessert! Many people think "cake" when they think of VeryVera, but our sweet tooth extends further than that. Inside this chapter, you'll find my take on classic dessert bars, along with a few other delectable treats. First, let's go over a few things.

PAN PREPARATION FOR BARS

All of our bar recipes are created with a half sheet pan with edges (13 x 18 inches) in mind. If you use this size pan, you'll end up with enough bars to serve your current purpose, plus enough to freeze or share as a gift!

When preparing the sheet pan, we use floured baking spray (PAM® or Baker's Joy®). If the recipe does not call for preparing the sheet pan with baking spray, you can use parchment paper to line the pan. Half sheet pan parchment liners can be purchased online. These are easy to use and make for easy cleanup. The bars featured in this chapter have been tested so as not to overflow the pan during baking. However, we do recommend putting foil under your pan on first use of a recipe, just to be safe.

BAKING

For any baked products, when the aroma from baking gets strong, check the oven. The product may be ready before your timer goes off, based on how your oven is calibrated. I also recommend setting the timer 10 minutes early to be safe if it's a recipe you haven't made before.

TOOLS AND EQUIPMENT

• **Sturdy rubber spatula**—It is extremely versatile in cooking and baking—great for mixing and folding ingredients.

• **Thin wooden spoon**—A good wooden spoon has a medium handle length and it is thin enough so you can "feel" in the pan when you are stirring. It is such a versatile tool!

• **Wire whisk**—There's nothing like a heavy-duty wire whisk.

• **Small metal icing spatula**—This is great to use for spreading ingredients, not just decorating a cake.

PEANUT BUTTER BARS

Some say peanut butter and jelly make the perfect pair, but I'm partial to peanut butter and chocolate. When we prepare desserts for guests during the golf tournament in Augusta, they always ask for seconds on these! The chopped peanuts add crunch and balance the sweetness of the chocolate. There are so many presentation ideas to up the "wow" factor with these squares, but honestly, right from your hand is BEST!

MAKES: APPROXIMATELY 100 (1-INCH) SQUARES | PREP TIME: 25 MINUTES | NO BAKING

CRUST

Floured baking spray

2½ cups unsalted butter

7½ cups graham cracker crumbs

4 cups confectioners' sugar

3 cups Jif® creamy peanut butter*

TOPPING

1 (12-ounce) bag Hershey's® semi-sweet chocolate chips, approximately 2 cups

1½ cups Jif® creamy peanut butter

1 cup salted, roasted peanuts, chopped

1. Grease a half sheet pan (13 x 18 inches), with edges, with floured baking spray.

2. Melt the butter in the microwave in 20-second intervals.

3. In a large bowl, mix together the graham cracker crumbs and confectioners' sugar.

4. Add the melted butter and 3 cups of peanut butter to the bowl and mix until well blended.

5. Pat the crust mixture evenly into the greased half sheet pan.

6. Place in the freezer for at least 5 minutes.

TOPPING

1. In a large bowl, melt the chocolate chips in the microwave in 10-second intervals, stirring after each interval.

2. Stir in 1½ cups of peanut butter.

3. Pull the chilled crust out of the freezer.

4. Spread the melted chocolate mixture over the top of the crust.

5. Sprinkle the peanuts on top of the chocolate mixture.

6. Place in the refrigerator overnight to become firm.

7. Let the bars come to room temperature and cut into 1-inch squares.

*NOTE: THE FULL RECIPE WILL USE ALMOST AN ENTIRE 2½-POUND JAR OF JIF® PEANUT BUTTER.

lemon bars

Vera, my grandmother, was quite the hostess. She was known for having friends in for teas and special celebrations. The crystal sandwich platter (pictured right) was hers. The lemon bars would shine like the sun from her dining room table. They are the perfect balance of sweet and tart and are great in the afternoon or following a heavy meal.

MAKES: APPROXIMATELY 100 (1-INCH) SQUARES | PREP TIME: 45 MINUTES | BAKE TIME: 35 TO 45 MINUTES

COOKIE BASE

FLOURED BAKING SPRAY

4 STICKS UNSALTED BUTTER

1 CUP CONFECTIONERS' SUGAR, PLUS MORE FOR GARNISH

4 CUPS ALL-PURPOSE FLOUR

LEMON FILLING

4 CUPS GRANULATED SUGAR

½ CUP ALL-PURPOSE FLOUR

1 TEASPOON BAKING POWDER

8 LARGE EGGS, BEATEN

¾ CUP FRESHLY SQUEEZED LEMON JUICE

1 TEASPOON LEMON ZEST

1. Preheat the oven to 350°F, and grease a half sheet pan (13 x 18 inches), with edges, with floured baking spray.

2. Melt the butter in a large bowl in the microwave.

3. Add the confectioners' sugar and flour to the melted butter and mix until well blended.

4. Press into the greased half sheet pan.

5. Bake the cookie base for 15 to 20 minutes or until golden brown.

6. While the crust is baking, make the lemon filling; stir together the sugar, flour, and baking powder in a large bowl.

7. Add the eggs, lemon juice, and lemon zest and mix until well blended.

8. Pour the mixture over the hot crust and bake for another 20 to 25 minutes.

9. Let the bars cool completely.

10. Sprinkle with confectioners' sugar and cut into 1-inch squares.

NOTE: THIS PAN WILL BE VERY FULL AND THE LEMON FILLING WILL GO TO THE TOP OF THE PAN. BE VERY CAREFUL WHEN PLACING THE PAN IN THE OVEN FOR THE SECOND BAKE. THE HALF SHEET PAN IS THE PERFECT HEIGHT FOR LEMON BARS, BUT I ALSO SUGGEST ALUMINUM FOIL ON THE RACK BELOW THE PAN IN THE OVEN IN CASE IT SPILLS OVER.

HELLO DOLLIES

This simple and decadent dessert is sure to be a crowd pleaser. In fact, at VeryVera catered parties, this was more popular than the shrimp! Some say the recipe comes from the can of sweetened condensed milk, and others say it was made popular when the recipe was published during the time the musical Hello, Dolly! was on Broadway. Also known as Seven Layer Bars, these sweet treats are so rich, you'll want to cut them into small squares. When they come out of the oven, try resisting the urge to dive right in. They're best when cooled and set!

MAKES: APPROXIMATELY 100 (1-INCH) SQUARES | PREP TIME: 15 MINUTES | BAKE TIME: 35 MINUTES

Floured baking spray

1 cup unsalted butter, melted

3 cups graham cracker crumbs

2½ cups shredded coconut

1 (11-ounce) bag Hershey's® butterscotch chips, approximately 1¾ cups

1 (12-ounce) bag Hershey's semi-sweet chocolate chips, approximately 2 cups

2½ cups pecans, chopped

2 (14-ounce) cans sweetened condensed milk

1. Preheat the oven to 325°F and grease a half sheet pan (13 x 18 inches), with edges, with floured baking spray.

2. Melt the butter in a large bowl in the microwave.

3. Add the graham cracker crumbs to the melted butter and mix well by hand.

4. Once the graham cracker crumbs are moistened by the butter, press the mixture into the bottom of the prepared pan.

5. Layer the shredded coconut, butterscotch chips, chocolate chips, and pecans over the top.

6. Pour the sweetened condensed milk over the entire pan. Do not mix.

7. Bake for 35 minutes.

8. Cool completely before cutting into 1-inch squares.

NOTE: POP SOME IN THE FREEZER. YOU WILL HAVE DESSERT READY FOR THE NEXT OCCASION OR TO TAKE A TREAT TO WORK!

white chocolate raspberry bars

Looking for something new to take to Sunday's dinner on the grounds? These bars look great and taste even better. Sweet white chocolate mingles with slightly tart raspberry jam for the perfect balance of flavor. Toasted almonds add crunch and texture to complete the ensemble! The name itself always added sass to menu planning at VeryVera.

MAKES: 30 (2-INCH) SQUARES | PREP TIME: 35 MINUTES | BAKE TIME: 25 TO 30 MINUTES

FLOURED BAKING SPRAY

3 STICKS UNSALTED BUTTER

3 CUPS HERSHEY'S® PREMIER WHITE CHIPS, DIVIDED

3 LARGE EGGS

1½ CUPS GRANULATED SUGAR

3 CUPS ALL-PURPOSE FLOUR

1½ TEASPOONS SALT

1 TEASPOON ALMOND FLAVORING

1½ CUPS RASPBERRY JAM

1 CUP SLICED ALMONDS

1. Preheat the oven to 325°F and grease a half sheet pan (13 x 18 inches), with edges, with floured baking spray.

2. In a large bowl, melt the butter in the microwave.

3. Add half of the white chocolate chips to the melted butter. Set aside and do not stir the mixture.

4. In a mixer, beat the eggs on medium speed until foamy.

5. Gradually add the sugar, beating on medium speed until the mixture is creamy. Stir in the white chocolate chip mixture.

6. Add the flour, salt, and almond flavoring, mixing at low speed until just blended.

7. Spread ¾ of the batter into the prepared pan. Set the remaining batter aside.

8. Bake for 10 to 12 minutes or until lightly brown.

9. Stir the remaining white chocolate chips into the remaining batter and set aside.

10. Warm the raspberry jam and spread evenly over the warm baked crust.

11. Gently drop tablespoons of the remaining batter over the fruit spread. Swirl with a metal spreader to even out until a little raspberry jam is peeking through all over. Sprinkle with the sliced almonds.

12. Place back in the oven for an additional 15 to 20 minutes or until a toothpick comes out clean.

13. Cool completely and cut into 2-inch squares.

CHEESECAKE BROWNIES

Being the middle of five children, I had to show off to get attention. These brownies do just that when compared to other brownie recipes. The swirl is a real show stopper and the flavor is over the top.

MAKES: 30 (2-INCH) SQUARES | PREP TIME: 45 MINUTES | BAKE TIME: 35 MINUTES

CREAM CHEESE MIXTURE

4 ounces cream cheese, at room temperature

3 tablespoons unsalted butter, at room temperature

1/3 cup granulated sugar

1 large egg

2½ tablespoons self-rising flour

1 tablespoon almond extract*

BROWNIE MIXTURE

Floured baking spray

10 large eggs

5 cups granulated sugar

2½ cups all-purpose flour

2¾ cups Hershey's® cocoa powder

1¼ teaspoons salt

2½ cups unsalted butter, melted

2½ teaspoons pure vanilla extract

1. Preheat the oven to 325°F.

2. With a mixer on medium speed, beat the cream cheese, butter, and sugar until creamy, about 3 minutes.

3. Add the egg and beat well.

4. Scrape the sides of the bowl and continue to beat until well blended.

5. Add in the flour and almond extract and beat until well blended. Set aside.

6. To start on brownie mixture, grease a half sheet pan (13 x 18 inches), with edges, with floured baking spray.

7. In a clean bowl, beat the eggs with a mixer on medium speed, until creamy, about 3 minutes.

8. Add the sugar slowly, beating thoroughly after each addition. Beat for about 3 minutes.

9. Scrape the sides of the bowl very well.

10. Add the flour, cocoa, and salt and beat well.

11. Add the melted butter and vanilla extract.

12. Beat just until well blended, but don't overmix the batter.

13. Pour the brownie batter into the bottom of the prepared pan.

14. Dollop the cream cheese mixture on top of the brownie batter.

15. Using a knife or metal spatula, swirl the brownie batter and the cream cheese mixture.

16. Bake for 35 minutes or until the cream cheese mixture starts to brown slightly.

17. Cool completely before cutting into 2-inch squares.

*NOTE: DON'T BE SURPRISED AT THE PROPORTION OF ALMOND EXTRACT IN THE CREAM CHEESE MIXTURE. THE CONCENTRATION IS DISTRIBUTED THROUGHOUT THE ENTIRE PAN.

PEACH COBBLER

I love being referred to as a "Georgia peach"! I especially love serving this dessert when Georgia and South Carolina peaches are at their best, around July and August. Fresh peaches make all the difference in this classic Southern dessert. I suggest freezing fresh peach slices when they are in season so you can prepare this dish any time of the year. If fresh peaches are not available, opt for the frozen variety in your grocery freezer section rather than canned.

SERVES: 10 TO 12 | PREP TIME: 20 TO 25 MINUTES | BAKE TIME: 30 TO 35 MINUTES

1 stick unsalted butter

1 cup granulated sugar, plus more for peaches

1 cup self-rising flour

1 cup whole milk

½ teaspoon pure vanilla extract

¼ teaspoon almond extract

5 to 6 cups fresh peaches, peeled, thinly sliced, and lightly sugared

1. Preheat the oven to 350°F.

2. Melt the butter in a 10-inch cast-iron skillet in the preheating oven.

3. In a large bowl, mix together the sugar, flour, milk, and flavorings.

4. Pour the batter into the skillet with the melted butter.

5. Drain the excess peach juice from the peach slices.

6. Spoon the peaches on top of the batter in the skillet.

7. Bake for 30 to 35 minutes or until golden brown.

8. Serve warm with vanilla ice cream.

NOTE: TO FREEZE FRESH PEACHES, PEEL AND SLICE THE FRUIT. IN A BOWL, MIX THE PEACH SLICES WITH ENOUGH SUGAR TO LIGHTLY COVER THE PEACHES, ALONG WITH THE JUICE OF HALF A LEMON. LAY THE PEACH SLICES ON A SHEET PAN AND PLACE IN THE FREEZER. ONCE THE SLICES ARE FROZEN, YOU CAN STORE THEM IN A RESEALABLE PLASTIC BAG IN THE FREEZER. I RECOMMEND FREEZING THE AMOUNT OF PEACHES FOR THIS RECIPE AND MARKING ON THE PACKAGE ACCORDINGLY.

PECAN SANDIES

My grandmother called these Pecan Crescents and shaped them as the name implied. The mail-order version took a "safer" shape for shipping purposes but kept the same unbeatable taste. These tiny cookies melt in your mouth, so good luck trying to eat just one. They are highly addictive. Don't say I didn't warn you…

MAKES: APPROXIMATELY 140 BITE-SIZED COOKIES | PREP TIME: 45 MINUTES TO 1 HOUR | BAKE TIME: 50 MINUTES

1 cup margarine, at room temperature

½ cup granulated sugar, plus more for rolling

2 cups all-purpose flour

2 cups pecan meal*

½ teaspoon pure vanilla extract

⅛ teaspoon almond extract

1. Preheat the oven to 275°F and line a sheet pan with parchment paper.

2. In a mixer, cream the margarine on medium speed

3. Slowly add the sugar. Beat until light and fluffy, about 2 minutes.

4. Scrape the sides and bottom of the bowl well.

5. Add the flour, pecan meal, and flavorings. Mix until well blended.

6. Refrigerate the dough for several hours or overnight.

7. Pinch off pieces of the dough and shape into small rounds, about the size of a marble. Be sure to leave space between the cookies on the sheet pan.

8. Press the dough rounds flat, about the size of a quarter.

9. Bake for 20 minutes.

10. Once they are out of the oven and cool enough to handle, roll in granulated sugar, shaking off excess sugar gently.

11. Place the cookies back on the sheet pan.

12. Place in the oven and bake for an additional 30 minutes or until the cookies are golden brown and have a great toasted pecan aroma.

*NOTE: PECAN MEAL IS A SPECIALTY PRODUCT AND IN CERTAIN AREAS IT MAY BE DIFFICULT TO FIND. YOU CAN GRIND THE PECANS YOURSELF IN A FOOD PROCESSOR, PULSING QUICKLY AND WORKING WITH SMALL AMOUNTS AT A TIME. THE COOKIES WILL HAVE THE SAME FLAVOR BUT WILL BE SLIGHTLY SOFTER IN TEXTURE.

FEATURED IN *Flavor of Georgia submission – Honorable Mention,* New York Times

pecan bread pudding with bourbon sauce

Our mail-order division had several dessert items, and this one proved year after year to be a best seller! This decadent dessert was one chosen by Costco to sell in Southeastern division stores. We used day-old croissants from our Café to make this sweet staple. We added bourbon sauce for the "adult" version and sales went through the roof. For extra decadence, top with whipped cream or vanilla ice cream.

SERVES: 8 TO 10 | PREP TIME: 15 TO 20 MINUTES | BAKE TIME: 30 TO 40 MINUTES

BREAD PUDDING

FLOURED BAKING SPRAY

4 TABLESPOONS UNSALTED BUTTER

1 CUP GRANULATED SUGAR

3 LARGE EGGS, AT ROOM TEMPERATURE

1 CUP WHOLE MILK, AT ROOM TEMPERATURE

1 TABLESPOON PURE VANILLA EXTRACT

½ TEASPOON GROUND CINNAMON

⅛ TEASPOON GROUND NUTMEG

4 LARGE CROISSANTS

½ CUP PECAN PIECES

1. Preheat the oven to 350°F.

2. Grease an 8 x 8-inch casserole dish with floured baking spray and set aside.

3. Melt 4 tablespoons of butter in the microwave.

4. In a mixer, beat the melted butter and sugar until creamy.

5. Add the eggs, milk, vanilla, cinnamon, and nutmeg to the mixer. Beat until well blended.

6. Tear the croissants into 1-inch pieces and layer in the bottom of the prepared pan.

7. Pour the egg mixture over the croissants and soak for 5 to 10 minutes. You will need to push the croissant pieces down during this time to ensure even coverage.

8. After the bread has soaked in the egg mixture, sprinkle the pecan pieces over the bread.

9. Cover the pan with foil and bake for 25 to 30 minutes.

10. Remove the foil and bake for an additional 5 to 10 minutes to brown the top.

BOURBON SAUCE

6 TABLESPOONS UNSALTED BUTTER

¾ CUP DARK BROWN SUGAR, PACKED

2 TABLESPOONS BOURBON

bourbon sauce

1. Melt 6 tablespoons of butter in a medium saucepan over medium heat.

2. Add the brown sugar to the melted butter and stir until dissolved.

3. Remove from heat and stir in the bourbon.

4. Before serving, pour the sauce over the warm bread pudding and top with whipped cream or vanilla ice cream.

NOTE: OUR FIRST ORDER FOR COSTCO WAS FOR 10,000 UNITS OF BREAD PUDDING. WHEN WE HANDED OUT SAMPLES IN THE STORES, NO ONE EVER TURNED IT DOWN! TRY THIS RECIPE AND YOU'LL KNOW WHY.

CHAPTER 7

pound
CAKES

*P*ound cakes are a great overall dessert. They can be enjoyed for breakfast, lunch, or dinner. A slice of pound cake is just as appropriate eaten by hand from a napkin as it is on the finest dessert plate.

CONVENTION VS. CONVECTION

A lot of ovens today offer the option of convection bake. Convection allows you to bake evenly on multiple racks instead of just on the middle rack. If your oven has the convection setting and you choose to use it, lower the baking temperature by 25°F. If you are using a conventional oven and need to use more than the middle rack, rotate the pans so they bake evenly.

choosing your ingredients

BUTTER, MILK, AND EGGS

All the baked goods in this chapter will use unsalted butter, whole milk or heavy cream, and large eggs. Use unsalted butter so you can control the amount of salt in the recipe. If you do use salted butter, try cutting down on the other added salt by half. You always want your butter and eggs to be room temperature. Cold ingredients won't trap and hold air bubbles, which is what helps a cake rise. Let the butter sit at room temperature for at least an hour before beginning. To quickly warm cold eggs, place the whole eggs in a bowl of hot tap water for 10 minutes. Be careful not to leave the eggs in for too long, as they may begin to cook in the hot water.

FLOUR

At VeryVera, we were known for our light and fluffy cakes. To ensure the right texture of the cake, use cake flour. Cake flour has less protein than all-purpose flour. Less protein means less gluten, which will create a lighter and fluffier cake. Too much gluten can make a cake tough and rubbery. Cake flour is also pre-sifted, which contributes to the cake's texture. If you do not have cake flour, all-purpose flour can be substituted with this simple trick. Measure out 1 cup of all-purpose flour and then remove 2 tablespoons. Add 2 tablespoons of cornstarch and sift the mixture at least 5 times. Although I do suggest using real cake flour, this method can be used in a bind.

Generally, I recommend having every ingredient measured before you start on the first step. I make an exception for pound cakes since the butter and sugar cream for so long. Get those two ingredients going in the stand mixer, and then move on to measuring your remaining ingredients.

PANS

It's key to use the properly sized pan for pound cakes. All of these recipes are baked in a 12-cup Bundt cake pan. I prefer one that is heavy and well seasoned. I highly recommend Nordic Ware® Bundt pans. It is also key that you prepare the pan with floured baking spray. This will help stop the cake from sticking when you flip it out of the pan. The batter should fill the pan to about 1 to $1\frac{1}{2}$ inches from the top of the pan. If you overfill the pan, the cake will rise above the top edge of the pan, leaving a large crust. Use any extra batter to make muffins.

If you would like to use a smaller pan, I suggest using 6-cup Bundt pans. One pound cake recipe will fill two 6-cup Bundt pans. The batter should fill each pan to about $\frac{3}{4}$ to 1 inch from the top. These cakes will bake for 1 hour.

GLAZES

We know you'll want to make these pound cakes again after you try them for the first time, so each glaze recipe makes enough for two cakes. Pound cake glazes should be stored in the refrigerator until ready to use. The glaze will need to come to room temperature and may need to be microwaved to ensure the best consistency for glazing. To glaze a pound cake, use a pastry brush to lightly stroke the tops and the sides. Do not soak the cake with glaze.

SERVING AND STORAGE

Allow slices to come to room temperature before serving, or heat in the microwave for 20 seconds. To freeze for later, wrap the cake tightly in plastic wrap and place in an airtight container in the freezer. Pound cakes will last in the freezer for up to 6 months.

HISTORY LESSON

Pound cakes are what started my mail-order business. In my early days as a caterer in Augusta, I was asked to cater a wake for a family with very few connections in town. This experience made me realize that there wasn't currently a market to buy homemade food items via mail order. Eventually, this idea evolved into our mail-order division, and we began shipping pound cakes perfect for birthday celebrations, holiday gatherings, or sympathy gifts.

BITSY'S AMARETTO CAKE

This cake boasts a refined taste befitting the poise of my eldest sister, Bitsy. When Bitsy tested the recipe she said, "In our family, food is love—the reassuring, familiar, delicious treat or a cherished culinary tradition. While preparing 'my cake,' I couldn't help but wonder, 'Which tradition will this cake become in our family and which will it become in yours?'"

SERVES: 24 | PREP TIME: 30 TO 35 MINUTES | BAKE TIME: 1 HOUR AND 10 MINUTES

1 cup unsalted butter, at room temperature

3 cups granulated sugar

1 cup heavy cream, at room temperature

1½ teaspoons almond extract

⅓ cup amaretto liqueur

3 cups cake flour

¼ teaspoon salt

6 large eggs, at room temperature

Floured baking spray

GLAZE

2½ tablespoons unsalted butter

¼ cup granulated sugar

1¼ tablespoons water

2 tablespoons amaretto liqueur

This cake is my son John's birthday cake. During his first semester at the University of Georgia, one of his hall mates spotted a VeryVera can in his room. He excitedly said, "Hey! My mom orders from VeryVera!" John replied, "My mom IS VeryVera!"

1. Preheat the oven to 325°F.

2. Cream the butter and sugar in a large bowl of a stand mixer fitted with the paddle attachment on medium speed for 20 minutes, until light and fluffy.

3. While the butter and sugar are creaming, measure out the remaining ingredients for the pound cake.

4. In a liquid measuring cup, whisk together the cream, almond extract, and amaretto.

5. In another bowl, whisk together the cake flour and salt.

6. Once the butter and sugar have finished creaming, scrape the sides and bottom of the bowl.

7. With the mixer on low speed, add the eggs one at a time, beating well after each addition.

8. Scrape the sides and bottom of the bowl again.

9. Let the mixture beat on low speed for 5 minutes.

10. With the mixer still on low speed, alternately add the flour mixture and the cream mixture, beginning and ending with the flour mixture. Mix until well blended.

11. Scrape the bowl and incorporate any unmixed batter if necessary.

12. Prepare a large 12-cup Bundt pan with floured baking spray.

13. Pour the batter into the prepared Bundt pan until it is about 1 to 1½ inches from the top. Tap the pan on the counter to ensure there are no air bubbles. (If there is remaining batter, use it to make muffins.)

14. Bake for 1 hour and 10 minutes. Insert a wooden skewer into the cake, and if there is no cake on the skewer, it is done.

15. While the cake is in the oven, prepare the glaze (below).

16. Remove the cake from the oven. Allow the cake to cool in the pan, on a wire rack, for 15 minutes or until cool enough to handle with pot holders. Place the wire rack on top of the cake pan and flip the pan over. Gently lift the pan, being careful not to remove any of the outside crust.

17. Using a pastry brush, generously douse the curved top of the cake with glaze. The cake should appear shiny with the glaze but not saturated. This should dry in about 30 minutes and then you can wrap the cake. Any leftover glaze can be refrigerated for up to 2 weeks.

GLAZE

1. Melt the butter and sugar in a medium saucepan over medium heat.

2. Add the water and bring to a boil. Cook for 2 to 3 minutes or until the mixture is smooth and not grainy.

3. Remove from the heat and stir in the amaretto until well blended.

NOTE: THIS CAKE WAS ENJOYED ALL OVER THE U.S. BY HSN.COM CUSTOMERS.

lou's poppy seed cake

You'll find that Lou is the only sibling with two pound cakes. Why? Well, funny story . . . We started getting calls from customers who loved this cake but wanted us to know that poppy seed consumption can cause you to fail a drug test! Because we loved our customers and wanted them to keep their jobs, we replaced this cake with Lou's Cream Cheese Cake (page 166). Since it is such a delicious cake, though, I knew I couldn't leave it out of this book. Just . . . maybe eat it on the weekend and let your boss know ahead of time.

SERVES: 24 | PREP TIME: 30 TO 35 MINUTES | BAKE TIME: 1 HOUR AND 20 MINUTES

1 CUP UNSALTED BUTTER, AT ROOM TEMPERATURE

3 CUPS GRANULATED SUGAR

3 CUPS CAKE FLOUR

¼ TEASPOON BAKING SODA

6 LARGE EGGS, AT ROOM TEMPERATURE

1 CUP SOUR CREAM

2 TEASPOONS LEMON EXTRACT

2 TEASPOONS BUTTER FLAVOR

1 TEASPOON COCONUT FLAVOR

1 TEASPOON ORANGE FLAVOR

1 TEASPOON ALMOND FLAVOR

¼ CUP POPPY SEEDS

FLOURED BAKING SPRAY

1. Preheat the oven to 325°F.

2. Cream the butter and sugar in a large bowl of a stand mixer fitted with the paddle attachment on medium speed for 20 minutes, or until light and fluffy. Scrape the sides and bottom of the bowl.

3. While the butter and sugar are creaming, measure out the remaining ingredients for the pound cake.

4. In a large bowl, whisk together the cake flour and baking soda.

5. With the mixer on low speed, add the eggs one at a time, alternating with the dry ingredients.

6. Scrape the sides and bottom of the bowl again.

7. Let the mixer beat on low speed for 5 minutes.

8. Add the sour cream and flavorings. Beat until incorporated.

9. Add the poppy seeds and beat until just incorporated.

10. Scrape the sides of the bowl and incorporate any unmixed batter if necessary.

11. Prepare a large 12-cup Bundt pan with floured baking spray.

12. Pour the batter into the prepared Bundt pan until it is about 1 to 1½ inches from the top. Tap the pan on the counter to ensure there are no air bubbles. (If there is remaining batter, use it to make muffins.)

CONTINUED ON 171

TRIP'S LEMON CRISP CAKE

The Lemon Crisp Cake was named after my brother Trip. When Trip tested the recipe he said, "I have never made a cake from scratch! Had fun and I'm very happy with the results!" Each lemon-shocked bite makes this cake the perfect dessert for spring or summertime. This recipe uses both lemon extract and fresh lemon zest for a strong (not overpowering) lemon flavor. The glaze maintains the balance of sweet and sour that makes this cake so delicious!

SERVES: 24 | PREP TIME: 30 TO 35 MINUTES | BAKE TIME: 1 HOUR AND 20 MINUTES

1 cup unsalted butter, at room temperature

3 cups granulated sugar

1 cup heavy cream, at room temperature

1½ teaspoons pure vanilla extract

1 tablespoon lemon extract

¾ teaspoon butter flavor

3 cups cake flour

½ teaspoon salt

6 large eggs, at room temperature

1½ teaspoons fresh lemon zest

Floured baking spray

GLAZE

¼ cup hand-squeezed lemon juice

½ cup granulated sugar

¼ teaspoon butter flavor

½ teaspoon lemon extract

1. Preheat the oven to 325°F.

2. Cream the butter and sugar in a large bowl of a stand mixer fitted with the paddle attachment on medium speed for 20 minutes, or until light and fluffy.

3. While the butter and sugar are creaming, measure out the remaining ingredients for the pound cake.

4. In a liquid measuring cup, whisk together the cream and flavorings.

5. Whisk together the cake flour and salt in a bowl and set aside.

6. Once the butter and sugar have finished creaming, scrape the sides and bottom of the mixing bowl.

7. Add the eggs one at a time with the mixer on low speed, beating well after each addition.

8. Scrape the sides and bottom of the bowl again.

9. Let the mixture beat on low speed for 5 minutes.

10. With the mixer still on low speed, alternately add the flour mixture and the cream mixture, beginning with the flour mixture and ending with the cream mixture. Mix until well blended.

11. Scrape the sides of the bowl and incorporate any unmixed batter if necessary.

12. Add the lemon zest and mix well.

13. Prepare a large 12-cup Bundt pan with floured baking spray.

14. Pour the batter into the prepared Bundt pan until it is about 1 to 1½ inches from the top. Tap the pan on the counter to ensure there are no air bubbles. (If there is remaining batter, use it to make muffins.)

15. Bake for 1 hour and 20 minutes. Insert a wooden skewer into the cake, and if there is no cake on the skewer, it is done.

CONTINUED ON 170

NOTE: THIS FAVORITE WAS SOLD ON HSN.COM.

peanut butter cake

This was our July Cake of the Month, and it was almost as good as fireworks to its fans. Classic peanut butter and peanut butter chips ensure salty, sweet pleasure in each bite. Serve with a scoop of chocolate ice cream and the perfect pair is back together again! Consider this as an option for your contribution to the summer family reunion.

SERVES: 24 | PREP TIME: 30 TO 35 MINUTES | BAKE TIME: 1 HOUR AND 20 MINUTES

1 CUP UNSALTED BUTTER, AT ROOM TEMPERATURE

3 CUPS GRANULATED SUGAR

½ CUP JIF® SMOOTH PEANUT BUTTER

1 CUP HEAVY CREAM, AT ROOM TEMPERATURE

1 TEASPOON PURE VANILLA EXTRACT

3 CUPS CAKE FLOUR

½ TEASPOON SALT

6 LARGE EGGS, AT ROOM TEMPERATURE

1 CUP REESE'S® PEANUT BUTTER CHIPS

FLOURED BAKING SPRAY

GLAZE

2 TABLESPOONS GRANULATED SUGAR

2 TABLESPOONS WATER

1 TABLESPOON PEANUT BUTTER

⅛ TEASPOON PURE VANILLA EXTRACT

⅛ TEASPOON BUTTER FLAVORING

1. Preheat the oven to 325°F.

2. Cream the butter, sugar, and peanut butter in a large bowl of a stand mixer fitted with the paddle attachment on medium speed for 20 minutes, or until light and fluffy.

3. While the butter, sugar, and peanut butter are creaming, measure out the remaining ingredients for the pound cake.

4. In a liquid measuring cup, whisk together the cream and vanilla extract.

5. Whisk together the cake flour and salt in a bowl and set aside.

6. Once the mixture has finished creaming, scrape the sides and bottom of the bowl.

7. Add the eggs one at a time with the mixer on low speed, beating well after each addition.

8. Scrape the sides and bottom of the bowl again.

9. Let the mixture beat on low speed for 5 minutes.

10. With the mixer still on low speed, alternately add the flour mixture and cream mixture, beginning with the flour mixture and ending with the cream mixture. Mix until well blended.

11. Scrape the sides and bottom of the bowl.

12. Add the peanut butter chips and mix on low speed until just combined.

13. Scrape the sides of the bowl and incorporate any unmixed batter if necessary.

14. Prepare a large 12-cup Bundt pan with floured baking spray.

15. Pour the batter into the prepared Bundt pan until it is about 1 to 1½ inches from the top. Tap the pan on the counter to ensure there are no air bubbles. (If there is remaining batter, use it to make muffins.)

16. Bake for 1 hour and 20 minutes. Insert a wooden skewer into the cake, and if there is no cake on the skewer, it is done.

17. While the cake is in the oven, prepare the glaze (page 171).

CONTINUED ON 171

BETTY'S CITRUS BLUEBERRY CAKE

Betty was my mother, and a cake that is sweet with a tart edge would speak to her personality. I inherited that style and her blue eyes, so there is a lot about this cake that I love.

SERVES: 24 | PREP TIME: 30 TO 35 MINUTES | BAKE TIME: 1 HOUR AND 20 MINUTES

1 cup unsalted butter,
at room temperature

3 cups granulated sugar

1 cup heavy cream, at room
temperature

2 teaspoons pure vanilla
extract

2 teaspoons lemon extract

2 teaspoons orange extract

3 cups cake flour
(plus more for dusting
blueberries)

½ teaspoon salt

6 large eggs, at room
temperature

1½ teaspoons orange zest

1½ cups frozen
blueberries

Floured baking
spray

GLAZE

2 tablespoons orange juice
concentrate

½ cup granulated
sugar

2 tablespoons water

¼ teaspoon butter
flavoring

¼ teaspoon orange
extract

¾ teaspoon orange zest

1. Preheat the oven to 325°F.

2. Cream the butter and sugar in a large bowl of a stand mixer fitted with the paddle attachment on medium speed for 20 minutes, or until light and fluffy.

3. While the butter and sugar are creaming, measure out the remaining ingredients for the pound cake.

4. In a liquid measuring cup, whisk together the cream, vanilla extract, lemon extract, and orange extract.

5. In another bowl, whisk together the cake flour and salt.

6. Once the butter and sugar have finished creaming, scrape the sides and bottom of the bowl.

7. With the mixer on low speed, add the eggs one at a time, beating well after each addition.

8. Scrape the sides and bottom of the bowl again.

9. Let the mixture beat on low speed for 5 minutes.

10. With the mixer still on low speed, alternately add the flour mixture and the cream mixture, beginning and ending with the flour mixture. Mix until well blended.

11. Scrape the sides of the bowl and incorporate any unmixed batter if necessary.

12. Add the orange zest and mix well. (You add this one last because it gets caught around the paddle, the longer it mixes.)

13. Place the blueberries in a bowl. Add about ¼ cup of cake flour and toss. This will help them from bleeding and sinking to the bottom of the cake.

14. Sift excess flour off the blueberries by hand and add the coated blueberries to the batter mixture. Fold in by hand, incorporating completely.

NOTE: THE BLUEBERRIES NEED TO BE AS FROZEN AS POSSIBLE. I RECOMMEND MEASURING THE BLUEBERRIES AND KEEPING THEM IN THE FREEZER UNTIL NEEDED.

15. Prepare a large 12-cup Bundt pan with floured baking spray.

16. Pour the batter into the prepared Bundt pan until it is about 1 to 1½ inches from the top. Tap the pan on the counter to ensure there are no air bubbles. (If there is remaining batter, use it to make muffins.)

17. Bake for 1 hour and 20 minutes. Insert a wooden skewer into the cake, and if there is no cake on the skewer, it is done.

18. While the cake is in the oven, prepare the glaze (p. 167).

CONTINUED ON 167

cinnamon nut cake

Our September Cake of the Month is a coffee cake in pound cake form, drizzled with cream cheese icing. A slice of Cinnamon Nut is perfect for a breakfast meeting, a Sunday school treat, or for the teachers' lounge. Even if you give away this cake as a gift, the extra batter will make 4 muffins for you to keep for yourself. You'll be begging to start your day with a slice of this cake and a steaming cup of coffee!

SERVES: 24 | PREP TIME: 30 TO 35 MINUTES | BAKE TIME: 1 HOUR AND 20 MINUTES

1½ CUPS UNSALTED BUTTER, AT ROOM TEMPERATURE

3 CUPS GRANULATED SUGAR

3 CUPS CAKE FLOUR

½ TEASPOON SALT

6 LARGE EGGS, AT ROOM TEMPERATURE

1 TEASPOON PURE VANILLA EXTRACT

1½ CUPS SOUR CREAM

FLOURED BAKING SPRAY

STREUSEL

1 CUP PECANS, CHOPPED

¼ CUP DARK BROWN SUGAR, PACKED

1 TABLESPOON GROUND CINNAMON

⅓ CUP CAKE FLOUR

¼ TEASPOON PURE VANILLA EXTRACT

ICING

¼ STICK UNSALTED BUTTER, AT ROOM TEMPERATURE

4 OUNCES CREAM CHEESE, AT ROOM TEMPERATURE

¾ TEASPOON PURE VANILLA EXTRACT

½ POUND CONFECTIONERS' SUGAR

1. Preheat the oven to 325°F.

2. Cream the butter and sugar in a large bowl of a stand mixer fitted with the paddle attachment on medium speed for 20 minutes, until light and fluffy.

3. While the butter and sugar are creaming, measure out the remaining ingredients for the pound cake and streusel.

4. In a separate bowl, whisk together the cake flour and salt and set aside.

5. Mix the streusel ingredients in a separate bowl and set aside.

6. Once the butter and sugar have finished creaming, scrape the sides and bottom of the bowl.

7. With the mixer on low speed, add the eggs one at a time, beating well after each addition.

8. Scrape the sides and bottom of the bowl again.

9. Add the vanilla extract and let the mixture beat on low speed for 5 minutes.

10. With the mixer still on low speed, alternately add the flour mixture and sour cream, beginning with the flour mixture and ending with the sour cream. Mix until well blended.

11. Add ⅔ cup of streusel to the batter and mix on low speed until well blended.

12. Scrape the sides of the bowl and incorporate any unmixed batter if necessary.

13. Fold in the remaining streusel by hand.

14. Prepare a large 12-cup Bundt pan with floured baking spray.

15. Pour the batter into the prepared Bundt pan until it is about 1 to 1½ inches from the top. Tap the pan on the counter to ensure there are no air bubbles. (Use the remaining batter to make muffins. This should fill about 4 muffin cups.)

CONTINUED ON 170

SERVING SUGGESTION *This pound cake is best when warm. Heat a slice in the microwave for about 20 seconds. This treat will taste like a delectable, warm cinnamon roll!*

RASPBERRY SWIRL CAKE

What cake would make you smile when it's 100°F in August? Designated as our August Cake of the Month, the Raspberry Swirl Cake truly made you do just that. The smell of raspberries when you opened the box right after delivery was second to the experience of the very first bite.

SERVES: 24 | PREP TIME: 30 TO 35 MINUTES | BAKE TIME: 1 HOUR AND 20 MINUTES

1 cup unsalted butter, at room temperature

3 cups granulated sugar

¾ cup heavy cream, at room temperature

1 tablespoon pure vanilla extract

1 tablespoon lemon extract

¼ cup Razzmatazz® (raspberry liqueur)

3 cups cake flour

½ teaspoon salt

6 large eggs, at room temperature

½ cup raspberry pie filling

Floured baking spray

GLAZE

½ cup granulated sugar
1 tablespoon lemon juice

1 tablespoon water

½ teaspoon pure vanilla extract

⅛ teaspoon butter flavoring

1 tablespoon Razzmatazz®

1. Preheat the oven to 325°F.

2. Cream the butter and sugar in a large bowl of a stand mixer fitted with the paddle attachment on medium speed for 20 minutes, or until light and fluffy.

3. While the butter and sugar are creaming, measure out the remaining ingredients for the pound cake.

4. In a liquid measuring cup, whisk together the cream, flavorings, and Razzmatazz.

5. Whisk together the cake flour and salt in a bowl and set aside.

6. Once the butter and sugar have finished creaming, scrape the sides and bottom of the mixing bowl.

7. Add the eggs one at a time with the mixer on low speed, beating well after each addition.

8. Scrape the sides and bottom of the bowl again.

9. Let the mixture beat on low speed for 5 minutes.

10. With the mixer still on low speed, alternately add the flour mixture and cream mixture, beginning and ending with the flour mixture. Mix until well blended.

11. Scrape the sides of the bowl and incorporate any unmixed batter if necessary.

12. In a separate bowl, add 1 cup of batter to the raspberry pie filling and mix by hand until well blended.

13. Pour the filling mixture back into the mixing bowl with the remaining batter and swirl with a spatula. This process should take no more than 3 folds.

14. Prepare a large 12-cup Bundt pan with floured baking spray.

15. Pour the batter into the prepared Bundt pan until it is about 1 to 1½ inches from the top. Tap the pan on the counter to ensure there are no air bubbles. (If there is remaining batter, use it to make muffins.)

16. Bake for 1 hour and 20 minutes. Insert a wooden skewer into the cake, and if there is no cake on the skewer, it is done.

17. While the cake is in the oven, prepare the glaze (below).

18. Remove the cake from the oven. Allow the cake to cool in the pan, on a wire rack, for 15 minutes or until cool enough to handle with pot holders. Place the wire rack on top of the cake pan and flip the pan over. Gently lift the pan, being careful not to remove any of the outside crust.

19. Using a pastry brush, generously douse the curved top of the cake with glaze. The cake should appear shiny with the glaze but not saturated. This should dry in about 30 minutes and then you can wrap the cake. Any leftover glaze can be refrigerated for up to 2 weeks.

GLAZE

1. Combine the sugar, lemon juice, and water in a medium saucepan.

2. Cook over medium heat for 2 to 3 minutes or until the mixture is smooth and not grainy.

3. Remove from heat and add the flavorings and Razzmatazz. Stir until well blended.

vera's chocolate cake

I had to put my name on the chocolate pound cake! This recipe produces a cake so rich and decadent that it doesn't even need a glaze. The aroma of this pound cake while it's baking will have you going crazy waiting for it to come out of the oven. Stick it out—it will be worth it. If you want to "dress up the basic black dress," I've included an optional Kahlua® glaze. This will definitely impress your family and friends.

SERVES: 24 | PREP TIME: 30 TO 35 MINUTES | BAKE TIME: 1 HOUR AND 25 MINUTES

1 CUP UNSALTED BUTTER, AT ROOM TEMPERATURE

3 CUPS GRANULATED SUGAR

1½ CUPS BUTTERMILK, AT ROOM TEMPERATURE

2 TEASPOONS PURE VANILLA EXTRACT

2½ CUPS CAKE FLOUR

1 CUP HERSHEY'S® COCOA POWDER

1 TEASPOON SALT

½ TEASPOON BAKING POWDER

6 LARGE EGGS, AT ROOM TEMPERATURE

FLOURED BAKING SPRAY

GLAZE (OPTIONAL)

¼ CUP WATER

2 TABLESPOONS GRANULATED SUGAR

1 TABLESPOON KAHLUA®

1. Preheat the oven to 325°F .

2. Cream the butter and sugar in a large bowl of a stand mixer fitted with the paddle attachment on medium speed for 20 minutes, until light and fluffy.

3. While the butter and sugar are creaming, measure out the remaining ingredients for the pound cake.

4. In a liquid measuring cup, whisk together the buttermilk and vanilla extract.

5. In another bowl, whisk together the cake flour, cocoa powder, salt, and baking powder and set aside.

6. Once the butter and sugar have finished creaming, scrape the sides and bottom of the bowl.

7. With the mixer on low speed, add the eggs one at a time, beating well after each addition.

8. Scrape the sides and bottom of the bowl again.

9. Let the mixture beat on low speed for 5 minutes.

10. With the mixer still on low speed, alternately add the flour mixture and buttermilk mixture, beginning and ending with the flour mixture. Mix until well blended.

11. Scrape the sides of the bowl and incorporate any unmixed batter if necessary.

12. Prepare a large 12-cup Bundt pan with floured baking spray.

13. Pour the batter into the prepared Bundt pan until it is about 1 to 1½ inches from the top. Tap the pan on the counter to ensure there are no air bubbles. (If there is remaining batter, use it to make muffins.)

14. Bake for 1 hour and 25 minutes. Insert a wooden skewer into the cake, and if there is no cake on the skewer, it is done.

15. Remove the cake from the oven. Allow the cake to cool in the pan, on a wire rack, for 15 minutes or until cool enough to handle with pot holders. Place the wire rack on top of the cake pan and flip the pan over. Gently lift the pan, being careful not to remove any of the outside crust.

CONTINUED ON 169

HARRY'S OLD-FASHIONED CAKE

This recipe is the mother of all pound cakes. Don't let its simplicity fool you. No frills, just buttery, velvety cake goodness. Lemon and coconut brighten it up and keep it from being too heavy. This cake is named after my brother Harry and it has his seal of approval: "Our finished cake turned out tasting great! This recipe is exactly like the one she's been sending me for years!"

SERVES: 24 | PREP TIME: 30 TO 35 MINUTES | BAKE TIME: 1 HOUR AND 20 MINUTES

1 cup unsalted butter, at room temperature

3 cups granulated sugar

1 cup heavy cream, at room temperature

2 teaspoons pure vanilla extract

2 teaspoons lemon extract

2 teaspoons coconut flavoring

3 cups cake flour

½ teaspoon salt

6 large eggs, at room temperature

Floured baking spray

1. Preheat the oven to 325°F.

2. Cream the butter and sugar in a large bowl of a stand mixer fitted with the paddle attachment on medium speed for 20 minutes, or until light and fluffy.

3. While the butter and sugar are creaming, measure out the remaining ingredients for the pound cake.

4. In a large liquid measuring cup, whisk together the cream and flavorings and set aside.

5. Whisk together the cake flour and salt in a large bowl and set aside.

6. Once the butter and sugar have finished creaming, scrape the sides and bottom of the bowl.

7. Add the eggs one at a time with the mixer on low speed, beating well after each addition.

8. Scrape the sides and bottom of the bowl again.

9. Let the mixture beat on low speed for 5 minutes.

10. With the mixer still on low speed, add the flour mixture and the cream mixture alternately, beginning with flour mixture and ending with the cream mixture. Mix until well blended.

11. Scrape the sides of the bowl and incorporate any unmixed batter if necessary.

12. Prepare a large 12-cup Bundt pan with floured baking spray.

13. Pour the batter into the prepared Bundt pan until it is about 1 to 1½ inches from the top. Tap the pan on the counter to ensure there are no air bubbles. (If there is remaining batter, use it to make muffins.)

14. Bake for 1 hour and 20 minutes. Insert a wooden skewer into the cake, and if there is no cake on the skewer, it is done.

15. Remove the cake from the oven. Allow the cake to cool in the pan, on a wire rack, for 15 minutes or until cool enough to handle with pot holders. Place the wire rack on top of the cake pan and flip the pan over. Gently lift the pan, being careful not to remove any of the outside crust.

16. Allow the cake to cool completely before wrapping.

SERVING SUGGESTION

My son Cord says, "Heat up the griddle with butter and drop a slice of Harry's on top for the ultimate cake experience!"

chocolate chip cake

Our June Cake of the Month, this cake found its way to many Father's Day celebrations. What man doesn't love chocolate chip cookies? Our version finds all the flavors you want in a cookie in this sweet, playful cake! Who says you can't dunk a slice into a cold glass of milk?

SERVES: 24 | PREP TIME: 30 TO 35 MINUTES | BAKE TIME: 1 HOUR AND 20 MINUTES

1 CUP UNSALTED BUTTER, AT ROOM TEMPERATURE

3 CUPS GRANULATED SUGAR

8 OUNCES CREAM CHEESE, AT ROOM TEMPERATURE

⅛ TEASPOON SALT

¼ CUP HEAVY CREAM, AT ROOM TEMPERATURE

2 TEASPOONS PURE VANILLA EXTRACT

6 LARGE EGGS, AT ROOM TEMPERATURE

3 CUPS CAKE FLOUR

1¼ CUPS HERSHEY'S® MINI SEMI-SWEET CHOCOLATE CHIPS

FLOURED BAKING SPRAY

GLAZE

¼ CUP GRANULATED SUGAR

2 TABLESPOONS WATER

⅛ TEASPOON PURE VANILLA EXTRACT

⅛ TEASPOON CHOCOLATE FLAVORING

1. Preheat the oven to 325°F.

2. Cream the butter and sugar in a large bowl of a stand mixer fitted with the paddle attachment on medium speed for 20 minutes, or until light and fluffy.

3. While the butter and sugar are creaming, measure out the remaining ingredients for the pound cake.

4. After 20 minutes, add the cream cheese to the butter mixture and cream until light and fluffy, about 2 minutes.

5. Add the salt, cream, and vanilla and beat on medium speed until the ingredients are well incorporated.

6. Scrape the sides and bottom of the bowl.

7. With the mixer on low speed, add the eggs one at a time, beating well after each addition.

8. Scrape the sides and bottom of the bowl again.

9. Slowly add the cake flour and beat on low speed until well incorporated.

10. Scrape the sides of the bowl and incorporate any unmixed batter if necessary.

11. Add the chocolate chips and mix until just incorporated. Do not overmix.

12. Prepare a large 12-cup Bundt pan with floured baking spray.

13. Pour the batter into the prepared Bundt pan until it is about 1 to 1½ inches from the top. Tap the pan on the counter to ensure there are no air bubbles. (If there is remaining batter, use it to make muffins.)

14. Bake for 1 hour and 20 minutes. Insert a wooden skewer into the cake, and if there is no cake on the skewer, it is done.

15. While the cake is in the oven, prepare the glaze (page 171).

16. Remove the cake from the oven. Allow the cake to cool in the pan, on a wire rack, for 15 minutes or until cool enough to handle with pot holders. Place the wire rack on top of the cake pan and flip the pan over. Gently lift the pan, being careful not to remove any of the outside crust.

17. Using a pastry brush, generously douse the curved top of the cake with glaze. The cake should appear shiny with the glaze but not saturated. This should dry in about 30 minutes and then you can wrap the cake. Any leftover glaze can be refrigerated for up to two weeks.

CONTINUED ON 171

lou's cream cheese cake

This cake is my sister Lou's namesake. As with the other siblings, I asked Lou to test this recipe. The next day, she took the cake to work and received rave reviews from her coworkers! According to Lou, one man said the last time he'd tasted a cake like that was when his grandmother was still baking, and another swore it was the best pound cake he had ever tasted. What makes this cake unique is that it's baked in a cold oven. One of the simplest cakes, Lou's Cream Cheese is a classic. It has a flavor that will never go out of style!

SERVES: 24 | PREP TIME: 20 TO 25 MINUTES | BAKE TIME: 1 HOUR AND 25 MINUTES

1½ CUPS UNSALTED BUTTER, AT ROOM TEMPERATURE

3 CUPS GRANULATED SUGAR

8 OUNCES CREAM CHEESE, AT ROOM TEMPERATURE AND CUT INTO PIECES

6 LARGE EGGS, AT ROOM TEMPERATURE

¼ CUP HEAVY CREAM, AT ROOM TEMPERATURE

2 TEASPOONS PURE VANILLA EXTRACT

3 CUPS CAKE FLOUR

⅛ TEASPOON SALT

FLOURED BAKING SPRAY

1. *Do not preheat the oven.*

2. Cream the butter and sugar together in a large bowl of a stand mixer fitted with the paddle attachment on medium speed for 5 minutes.

3. Add the cream cheese to the butter mixture and cream until light and fluffy, about 2 minutes.

4. Scrape the sides and bottom of the bowl.

5. Add the eggs one at a time with the mixer on low speed, beating well after each addition.

6. Scrape the sides and bottom of the bowl again.

7. Let the mixture beat on low speed for 5 minutes.

8. In a separate bowl, whisk together the cream and vanilla extract.

9. In a large bowl, whisk together the cake flour and salt.

10. With the mixer still on low speed, alternately add the flour mixture and cream mixture, beginning with the flour mixture and ending with the cream mixture. Mix until well blended.

11. Scrape the sides of the bowl and incorporate any unmixed batter if necessary.

12. Prepare a large 12-cup Bundt pan with floured baking spray.

13. Pour the batter into the prepared Bundt pan until it is about 1 to $1\frac{1}{2}$ inches from the top. Tap the pan on the counter to ensure there are no air bubbles. (If there is remaining batter, use it to make muffins.)

14. Place the cake in a cold oven, then set the temperature to 300°F.

SERVING SUGGESTION

This pound cake is best enjoyed when warm. This can be done in the microwave, or you can lightly pan-fry a slice to get a nice crust on the outside.

15. Bake for 1 hour and 25 minutes. Insert a wooden skewer into the cake, and if there is no cake on the skewer, it is done.

16. Remove the pan from the oven, and immediately push down the sides if they have risen above the edge of the pan. This will keep the edges from getting crisp and separating when you invert the pan.

17. Allow the cake to cool in the pan, on a wire rack, for 15 minutes or until cool enough to handle with pot holders. Place the wire rack on top of the cake pan and flip the pan over. Gently lift the pan, being careful not to remove any of the outside crust.

18. Allow the cake to cool completely before wrapping.

BETTY'S CITRUS BLUEBERRY CAKE CONTINUED FROM 155

19. Remove the cake from the oven. Allow the cake to cool in the pan, on a wire rack, for 15 minutes or until cool enough to handle with pot holders. Place the wire rack on top of the cake pan and flip the pan over. Gently lift the pan, being careful not to remove any of the outside crust.

20. Using a pastry brush, generously douse the curved top of the cake with glaze. The cake should appear shiny with the glaze but not saturated. This should dry in about 30 minutes and then you can wrap the cake. Any leftover glaze can be refrigerated for up to 2 weeks.

GLAZE

1. Combine the orange juice concentrate, sugar, and water in a medium saucepan. Cook for 2 to 3 minutes over medium heat, or until the mixture is smooth and not grainy.

2. Add the flavorings and stir until well combined.

STORAGE NOTE *This cake must be refrigerated, due to the berries.*

georgia brandied peach cake

This cake was created to pay homage to the home state of VeryVera: Georgia. Many people begged for the recipe for this favorite, and until now, I have kept it a secret. I sent this cake as a gift to a business associate in Columbus, Georgia, a few years ago. His response was, "Peaches and brandy? Two of my favorite things!" I hope you enjoy this cake as much as he did!

SERVES: 24 | PREP TIME: 30 TO 35 MINUTES | BAKE TIME: 1 HOUR AND 20 MINUTES

1 CUP UNSALTED BUTTER, AT ROOM TEMPERATURE

3 CUPS GRANULATED SUGAR

⅓ CUP HEAVY CREAM, AT ROOM TEMPERATURE

1 TEASPOON PEACH FLAVOR*

¾ CUP PEACH SCHNAPPS

3 CUPS CAKE FLOUR

¼ TEASPOON SALT

6 LARGE EGGS, AT ROOM TEMPERATURE

FLOURED BAKING SPRAY

GLAZE

2 ½ TABLESPOONS UNSALTED BUTTER

¼ CUP GRANULATED SUGAR

1 ¼ TABLESPOONS WATER

2 TABLESPOONS PEACH SCHNAPPS

*IF YOU ARE UNABLE TO FIND PEACH FLAVORING IN YOUR LOCAL GROCERY STORE, WE RECOMMEND PURCHASING OLIVENATION-BRAND PEACH FLAVORING ONLINE.

1. Preheat the oven to 325°F.

2. Cream the butter and sugar in a large bowl of a stand mixer fitted with the paddle attachment on medium speed for 20 minutes, until light and fluffy.

3. While the butter and sugar are creaming, measure out the remaining ingredients for the pound cake.

4. In a large measuring cup, whisk together the cream, peach flavor, and peach schnapps.

5. In another bowl, whisk together the cake flour and salt.

6. Once the butter and sugar have finished creaming, scrape the sides and bottom of the bowl.

7. With the mixer on low speed, add the eggs one at a time, beating well after each addition.

8. Scrape the sides and bottom of the bowl again.

9. Let the mixture beat on low speed for 5 minutes.

10. With the mixer still on low speed, alternately add the flour mixture and the cream mixture, beginning with the flour mixture and ending with the cream mixture. Beat until well blended.

11. Scrape the sides of bowl and incorporate any unmixed batter if necessary.

12. Prepare a large 12-cup Bundt pan with floured baking spray.

13. Pour the batter into the prepared Bundt pan until it is about 1 to 1½ inches from the top. Tap the pan on the counter to ensure there are no air bubbles. (If there is remaining batter, use it to make muffins.)

14. Bake for 1 hour and 20 minutes. Insert a wooden skewer into the cake, and if there is no cake on the skewer, it is done.

15. While the cake is in the oven, prepare the glaze.

SERVING SUGGESTION *This is best served warm with a dollop of whipped cream.*

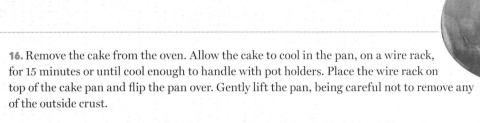

16. Remove the cake from the oven. Allow the cake to cool in the pan, on a wire rack, for 15 minutes or until cool enough to handle with pot holders. Place the wire rack on top of the cake pan and flip the pan over. Gently lift the pan, being careful not to remove any of the outside crust.

17. Using a pastry brush, generously douse the curved top of the cake with glaze. The cake should appear shiny with the glaze but not saturated. This should dry in about 30 minutes and then you can wrap the cake. Any leftover glaze can be refrigerated for up to 2 weeks.

glaze

1. Melt the butter and sugar in a medium saucepan over medium heat.

2. Add the water and bring to a boil. Cook for 2 to 3 minutes or until the mixture is smooth and not grainy.

3. Remove from heat and stir in schnapps until well blended.

VERA'S CHOCOLATE CAKE CONTINUED FROM 160

16. Allow the cake to cool completely before wrapping. If you choose to glaze the cake, the cake will still need to be warm when it is glazed.

GLAZE (OPTIONAL)

1. In a small pan over high heat, stir together the water and sugar. Bring to a full rolling boil.

2. Cover the pan and remove it from the heat. Let it cool slightly.

3. Add the Kahlua and stir until incorporated.

4. Using a pastry brush, generously douse the curved top of the cake with glaze. The cake should appear shiny with the glaze but not saturated. This should dry in about 30 minutes and then you can wrap the cake. Any leftover glaze can be refrigerated for up to 2 weeks.

SERVING SUGGESTION   *Present a slice of this decadent cake with a drizzle of caramel and a pinch of sea salt.*

TRIP'S LEMON CRISP CAKE CONTINUED FROM 151

16. While the cake is in the oven, prepare the glaze.

17. Remove the cake from the oven. Allow the cake to cool in the pan, on a wire rack, for 15 minutes or until cool enough to handle with pot holders. Place the wire rack on top of the cake pan and flip the pan over. Gently lift the pan, being careful not to remove any of the outside crust.

18. Using a pastry brush, generously douse the curved top of the cake with glaze. The cake should appear shiny with the glaze but not saturated. This should dry in about 30 minutes and then you can wrap the cake. Any leftover glaze can be refrigerated for up to 2 weeks.

GLAZE

1. Combine all the ingredients in a small bowl and mix with a wire whisk until well blended.

2. Whisk until the mixture is smooth and not grainy.

CINNAMON NUT CAKE CONTINUED FROM 156

16. Bake for 1 hour and 20 minutes. Insert a wooden skewer into the cake, and if there is no cake on the skewer, it is done.

17. Remove the cake from the oven. Allow the cake to cool in the pan, on a wire rack, for 15 minutes or until cool enough to handle with pot holders. Place the wire rack on top of the cake pan and flip the pan over. Gently lift the pan, being careful not to remove any of the outside crust.

18. Place the cake in the refrigerator to chill. While the cake is in the refrigerator, prepare the icing.

ICING

1. Cream the butter and cream cheese in the bowl of a stand mixer for 3 minutes. At the end of the 3 minutes, scrape the bowl extremely well.

2. Add the vanilla extract and beat for 1 to 2 minutes.

3. Slowly add the confectioners' sugar, about 1 cup at a time, beating on low to ensure the sugar does not fly out of the mixer.

4. After each addition of confectioners' sugar, scrape the bottom of the bowl extremely well.

5. Once all the confectioners' sugar is incorporated, beat on low speed for 3 minutes.

6. To ice the pound cake, heat the cream cheese icing in the microwave for about 45 seconds or until it is slightly warm.

7. Drizzle the warm icing over the top of the chilled cake. The cake should not be completely covered with icing. Once the cake is iced, place in the refrigerator until the icing is hardened.

8. Any leftover icing can be refrigerated for up to 2 weeks.

NOTE: THIS CAKE WAS ENJOYED ALL OVER THE U.S. BY COSTCO.COM CUSTOMERS.

PEANUT BUTTER CAKE CONTINUED FROM 152

18. Remove the cake from the oven. Allow the cake to cool in the pan, on a wire rack, for 15 minutes or until cool enough to handle with pot holders. Place the wire rack on top of the cake pan and flip the pan over. Gently lift the pan, being careful not to remove any of the outside crust.

19. Using a pastry brush, generously douse the curved top of the cake with glaze. The cake should appear shiny with the glaze but not saturated. This should dry in about 30 minutes and then you can wrap the cake. Any leftover glaze can be labeled and refrigerated for up to 2 weeks.

GLAZE

1. Stir together the sugar, water, and peanut butter in a medium saucepan over medium heat.

2. Cook for 2 to 3 minutes or until the mixture is smooth and not grainy.

3. Remove from heat and add the flavorings. Stir until well combined.

LOU'S POPPY SEED CAKE CONTINUED FROM 148

13. Bake for 1 hour and 20 minutes. Insert a wooden skewer into the cake, and if there is no cake on the skewer, it is done.

14. Remove the cake from the oven. Allow the cake to cool in the pan, on a wire rack, for 15 minutes or until cool enough to handle with pot holders. Place the wire rack on top of the cake pan and flip the pan over. Gently lift the pan, being careful not to remove any of the outside crust.

15. Allow the cake to cool completely before wrapping.

CHOCOLATE CHIP CAKE CONTINUED FROM 164

GLAZE

1. Combine the sugar and water in a medium saucepan. Cook for 2 to 3 minutes over medium heat, or until the mixture is smooth and not grainy.

2. Remove from the heat and add vanilla extract and chocolate flavoring.

SERVING SUGGESTION

If you don't want a glass of milk, this pound cake is also great when paired with vanilla ice cream and chocolate syrup.

NOTE: THIS RECIPE WAS ENJOYED ALL OVER THE U.S. BY COSTCO.COM CUSTOMERS.

recipes for your table

VeryVera was a great source for food "Just Like Mama Made It." Customers would tell us they transferred the dish from our disposable container to their own baking dish and just kept the VeryVera part to themselves. We were fine with that. Actually, what a compliment!

When I remember some of my favorite cookbooks along the way, as a newlywed and new hostess I truly loved the ones that put menus together for you and referenced where to find those recipes in the book. So, for old times' sake, I've decided to do that myself in hopes that the overall VeryVera experience described above can be yours, but this time you can say you made it yourself, with a straight face!

PRO TIP

Last tip of the book: Plan ahead! I have every one of my planners starting with 1984. Each page shows event dates, handwritten orders, and the steps I took each day to make it all happen. I still work from a planner and certainly try not to leave every detail to the last minute. Remember, the freezer is your friend, and foods that have a shelf life of several days can be made ahead.

sunday brunch

Chicken Poppyseed Casserole (page 93)

Tomato Pie (page 69)

Cheddar Cheese & Chive Biscuits stuffed with Ham (page 31)

Baked French Toast (page 80)

Fresh Fruit

Betty's Citrus Blueberry Pound Cake (page 155) or

Cinnamon Nut Pound Cake (page 156)

Sunday Brunch

CHICKEN POPPYSEED CASSEROLE (PAGE 93)

TOMATO PIE (PAGE 69)

CHEDDAR CHEESE & CHIVE BISCUITS
STUFFED WITH HAM (PAGE 31)

BAKED FRENCH TOAST (PAGE 80)

FRESH FRUIT

BETTY'S CITRUS BLUEBERRY POUND CAKE
(PAGE 155)

OR CINNAMON NUT POUND CAKE (PAGE 156)

sunday dinner or family-style supper

Bitsy's Meatloaf (page 91)

And/or

Chicken & Wild Rice Casserole (page 84)

Parmesan Squash Casserole (page 67)

Pasta Salad (page 72)

Creamed Spinach (page 72)

Green Beans

Yeast Rolls (page 40)

Carrot Cake (page 120) or Peach Cobbler (page 138)

summer celebration

Shrimp & Crawfish (page 88)

Vera's Salad (page 58)

Sour Cream Muffins (page 41)

Lemon Cake (page 110) or

Trip's Lemon Crisp Cake (page 151)

cocktail party

Cheese Straws (page 35)

Vidalia Onion Dip (page 32)

Honey Pecan Spread on Ginger Snaps with Fig Preserves (page 39)

Bacon-Tomato Spread on Toasted Rounds (page 39)

—COCKTAIL SANDWICHES—

Mama's Egg Salad (page 47) Pimento Cheese (page 28)

Tuna Salad (page 60) Vera's Signature Chicken Salad (page 50)

Bitsy's Meatloaf Sliders (page 91)

Roasted Tomato Basil Shooters with Shrimp Garnish (page 54)

—DESSERTS—

Pecan Sandies (page 139)

White Chocolate Raspberry Bars (page 134)

Lemon Bars (page 130)

cocktail party
MENU

Cheese Straws (page 35)

Vidalia Onion Dip (page 32)

Honey Pecan Spread on Ginger Snaps
with Fig Preserves (page 39)

Bacon-Tomato Spread on Toasted Rounds (page 39)

Cocktail Sandwiches
Mama's Egg Salad (page 47)   Pimento Cheese (page 28)

Tuna Salad (page 60)
Vera's Signature Chicken Salad (page 50)

Bitsy's Meatloaf Sliders (page 91)

Roasted Tomato Basil Shooters
with Shrimp Garnish (page 54)

Pecan Sandies (page 139)

White Chocolate Raspberry Bars (page 134)

Lemon Bars (page 130)

southern dinner party

—FIRST COURSE—
Vidalia Onion Tartlets (page 32)
Pimento Cheese-Stuffed Celery Sticks (page 28)

—SECOND COURSE—
Butternut Squash Soup (page 57)

—THIRD COURSE—
Vera's Salad (page 58)

—MAIN COURSE—
Stacked Meatloaf:
Creamed Spinach (page 72)
Warm Potato Salad (page 70)
Bitsy's Meatloaf (page 91)
French-Fried Onions or Okra Fries
Sweet Potato Rolls (page 41) with
Honey Pecan Spread (page 39)

—DESSERT—
Pecan Bread Pudding
with Bourbon Sauce (page 140)

DINNER PART

Vidalia Onion Tartlets (page 32)

Pimento Cheese-Stuffed
Celery Sticks (page 28)

Butternut Squash Soup (page 57)

Vera's Salad (page 58)

Stacked Meatloaf
Creamed Spinach (page 72)
Warm Potato Salad (page 70)
Bitsy's Meatloaf (page 91)
French-Fried Onions or Okra Fries

Sweet Potato Rolls (page 41)
with Honey Pecan Spread (page 39)

Pecan Bread Pudding with Bourbon Sauce (page 140

I have given you my life in this book. My heart and soul are behind the name that everyone calls me, VeryVera. The support of innumerable people through the years has guided the process and kept me grounded.

First, I want to thank my family for their support and help during this entire process. My loving husband, Andy Kilpatrick, has been the perfect soulmate and has shown as much enthusiasm for this project as anyone. He's endured a lot of my "don't quit until it's done" scenarios in twenty-six years and has made the off times some of the greatest of my life. Thank you to my sons John and Daniel for encouraging me to continue to work hard and grow in my endeavors. Thank you for the time you spent at VeryVera from an early age. Thanks to both Mallory and Catherine for their time at VeryVera and the impact they made. Now as daughters-in-law, they have evaluated samples for almost everything in the book and have given me honest feedback. Thanks to my son Cord for making deliveries while home from college and for coining me "Granny V" when his daughter, Pinckney, was born. Thanks to my daughter-in-law Mary Margaret who

has such a sense of style and gives me great advice. Thanks to my daughter Currie for her time in the early development of our mail-order company, for her attention to special customers, and for the signature Currie earrings I wear all the time. Thanks to my son-in-law Brent who never fails to be one of the first to wish me "happy birthday" every year, thus making it easier to love a Florida Gator. Finally, thanks to my daughter Jessie for her time in our bakery, and to her husband, Allen, who trusted me with all the details of their wedding.

There never would have been a "VeryVera" if it wasn't for my grandmother, Vera Wright Wingfield, my mother, Betty Stewart Wingfield, and my mother-in-law, Sue Stewart. They taught me so much and helped make me the person I am today. I am appreciative of not only the lessons they taught me in the kitchen, but I also thank them for guiding me along the recipe of success, as ingredients from each of their personalities are in the person I have become.

Thank you to Charles Stewart for his support in the early developmental stages of VeryVera and to his wife, Rita, who has always been so supportive and helpful in anything that had to do with loving and caring for our children. Thank you to my siblings, Bitsy, Trip, Harry, and Lou, for recipe testing and approving their namesake pound cakes.

I want to extend endless thanks to the VeryVera family—to those who have stayed with me throughout

CLOCKWISE, FROM TOP LEFT: VERA AND HER HUSBAND ANDY; DANIEL, VERA, AND JOHN AT THE JUNIOR ACHIEVEMENT BUSINESS HALL OF FAME AWARD CEREMONY; RECIPE CARD FROM VERA'S MOTHER-IN-LAW, SUE STEWART; THE KILPATRICK/STEWART FAMILY.

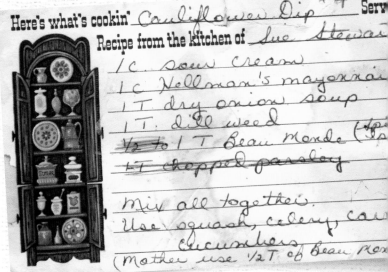

Here's what's cookin' *Cauliflower Dip* x 4 Serv
Recipe from the kitchen of *Sue Stewart*

1 C. sour cream
1 C. Hellman's mayonnaise
1 T. dry onion soup
1 T. dill weed
½ to 1 T Beau Monde (Sp
1 T chopped parsley

Mix all together.
Use squash, celery, cau
cucumbers
(Mother use ½ T of Beau Mon

the years and to those who helped build the VeryVera brand. From management, to high school employees, to seasonal staff, and even to campers that have traveled with us through the years, each has made their mark in their time with us. Special thanks to Christina Cannon and Melissa Carden, both of whom were so instrumental in the growth of VeryVera and were testers for the recipes in the book. Their attention to detail in the testing process gives me great confidence for each recipe. Many thanks to Donna Nail and Felicia Beale who seemed to, from memory, recite every detail of every recipe. Love and great thanks to Kitty Hopkins for inventing the "Kitty Swirl" that made our cakes so unique and to Rebecca Jefferson for her tried-and-true representation of the Kitty Swirl and her instruction to everyone who ever set foot in the bakery. Special recognition to Nick Thompson, our Mail Order Manager, who knew all the corporate customers by name, remembered every order they ever placed, and made his department work so flawlessly.

Thank you to Susan Ely, the manager and creator of our Gourmet to Go line, Peggy Engelke, our Bakery and Catering Director, and Terri Trowell, the very first employee of VeryVera who gave me twenty-one wonderful years. These three women helped put some of these recipes on the map. Thanks to DeDe Wilson and Katye Colbert for keeping VeryVera's finances in order and for their untold hours with me in support of the business as though it was their own. Thanks to Lecia Raiford and Andrew Jenkins, long-standing

members of our team, and especially to Julie Voegtlen, without whom I could never have slept a wink during the duration of my career.

Thanks to my Advisory Board that served three-year terms beginning in 1999 until we closed our retail operation in 2013. This group of twenty-five individuals had strong ties to our company as customers, community leaders, and entrepreneurs. These men and women volunteered to meet with me once a month for an hour in our building and allowed me to call on them for advice or suggestions when I needed them.

The book would not be what it is without our fabulous photographer, Peter Frank Edwards, and our amazing food stylist, Sandy Lang. We became friends instantly. Thank you for your beautiful work and all the care you put into each picture. Your refusal to stop before each shot was perfect let me know that we were meant to work together. Thank you to these Augusta, Georgia, antique stores; Mema Had One, Savvy Shopper, and Trends & Traditions. We appreciate your efforts in locating and researching the perfect pieces for our photography.

A big thank you to my mentors for the cookbook project: Virginia Willis, Matt and Ted Lee, and Sara

Foster. Thanks to my lifelong friend Debbie Tamplin for understanding very few calls and infrequent visits as I tried to keep a handle on my business and my family through the years and for helping with recipe testing.

Thank you to my team, Rachel Schifter, Project Manager, and Emily Yates, Creative Manager. You became part of VeryVera at the absolute perfect time in my career and hopefully yours. The long hours, trials, and challenges of this journey have been rewarding with you by my side. I truly would not be realizing this dream without you. Thanks to Haleigh Newman, who tackled any request and kept the kitchen pumping out the best tested recipes due to her attention to detail when prepping. Thank you to Ashley Fraxedas and everyone at Story Farm Publishing: Bob Morris, Lauren Eggert, and Karen Cakebread. Thank you to our Creative Firm, Wier/Stewart, for their input and enthusiasm in this project and the knowledge of our brand for many years. To Lauren Hopkins and Kari Torstenson of LBH &

Co., thank you for your encouragement and excitement for the cookbook and for getting it out to the world. I'm grateful for the magical way we came together.

Thank you to the editors and features editors in more than three dozen magazines who received packages from VeryVera through the years and were impressed enough to write about us. The introduction to so many of our customers came through that exposure and the result was critical to the growth of the company.

To all of my customers throughout the years of VeryVera, thank you for your interest and love of my company. Thank you for sharing VeryVera with your family, your associates, and your friends. Thank you for your endless word-of-mouth promotion of our company. I enjoyed serving your lunch, catering your many events, and sending you delicious treats in the mail. Thank you for your patience as I have worked for the last four years on this book. I hope you found it to be worth the wait!

CLOCKWISE, FROM TOP LEFT: KITTY HOPKINS; SANDY LANG AND VERA; THE VERYVERA CATERING TEAM; A VERYVERA CATERED EVENT; VERA, RACHEL SCHIFTER, AND EMILY YATES; VERYVERA PACKAGING; THE VERYVERA BUILDING AND CATERING VAN; VERA'S SIBLINGS, BITSY, TRIP, VERA, HARRY, AND LOU.

INDEX

PAGE NUMBERS IN ITALICS INDICATE PHOTOS.

VERA STEWART IS A WELL-KNOWN ENTREPRENEUR and businesswoman in Augusta, Georgia, thanks to her successful catering business, widely sold mail-order confections, summer cooking camp for children, and syndicated cooking and lifestyle show. Her leadership and business acumen have allowed her to mentor young people throughout her career, calling back to her origins as a home economics teacher. Today, *The VeryVera Show* is syndicated in several Eastern markets and VeryVera Cooking Camp is franchised to multiple cities outside of Augusta. Her accolades include Chamber of Commerce 1997 Small Business Person of the Year, CSRA Business Hall of Fame Laureate, two-time GABBY Merit Award winner, University of Georgia FACS Professional Achievement Award winner, and University of Georgia FACS 100 Honoree. Vera lives in Augusta with her husband, Andy, an attorney, and her growing family.

Vera Stewart

From the kitchen of

Lemon Cheese Eggs

2½ c. flour
1 c. pecans chopped
½ tsp. salt
½ tsp. grated lemon
rind

Serves

Hot Buttered Rum
Elizabeth Rick

REMINDERS

sticks butter, melt
½# Velveeta
cool & add 2 cans
crab & add 2 cans
8 oz. of butter melted

20 sl. white bread
rolled thin
spread crab mixture
on bread, roll up
then dip in butter &
roll in sesame seed
Freeze. Partially thaw
cut into
3-4 slices

Derby Pie
Betsy

room temperature
sugar
all-purpose flour
(1 stick) unsalted butter
chocolate chips
chopped pecans, lightly toasted
bourbon
1 t. vanilla
9-inch un...
whipped cream

Broccoli Casse
Vera Stewart

2 pkg. broccoli (frozen, cho
defrost & drain
Combine: 2 beaten eggs
3/4 c. mayonnai
1 c. grated
1 can cream

Put in
dish
45

Recipe from the kitchen of:

1 (No. 2) can French styl...
1 (No. 2) can English peas (an
1 small jar pimento (drain)
2 stalks celery, cut
1 bell pepper, cut
1 medium onion
(optional- cu

Rodney

Milky-Way Cake

Melt 4 milky ways in a double boiler,
with 1 stick margarine. keep warm
until the cake is mixed
1 stick margarine
2 cups sugar
4 eggs
1 cup buttermilk
½ t. soda
2 t. vanilla
1 c. chopped nuts

2 sticks oleo
⅛ tsp. red pepper
2 c. plain flour, unsifted
2 c. Rice Krispies
4 Rice Krispies
Combine cheese & oleo. Add flour, pepper
about the size of marble. Mix well
cookie sheet. Press with fork. Place on ungreased
for 15 min. Makes about
100 cookies.

Lace Cookies
Miriam B. Loo

½ cup white sugar
½ cups brown sugar
quick cooking oatmeal
salt
flour
beaten
½ teaspoon vanilla
Put foil on cookie sheet
Put 1 teaspoon of cookie
mixture in foil Press
a bit Bake 325

Here's what's cookin':
1½ lb. ground
¼ lb. hot saus
1 cup bread crum
1 egg
1½ t. salt
¼ t. pepper

Mix
an
a
ho
the

Here's what's cookin' Caramel Frosting Little Mullins
Recipe from the kitchen of
½ c butter
1 c. Brown sugar-dark
¼ c. milk
1½ to 2 c confectioners sugar
(sifted)
Melt butter, add brown sugar
Let bubble 2 min while stirring
add milk and bring to full boil
again. Cool and add conf.
sugar blending a little at a tim...

Instant Miracle

dry yeast
water
sifted self-
flour
sugar

Dissolve yeast in warm wate
flour sugar & soda. Cut in
buttermilk + yeast + mix. Pla
dough on floured surface.
biscuit cutter. Let warm
baking in oven 350°

Trim crusts from bread

Mix all above & spread on
bread - cut in strips

Freeze on cookie sheets
store in plastic bags

Bake 10 min. 400°

1 - Loaf b
½ - lb grat
6 - slices ch
1 - small pkg
1 - small onion
1 - cup
salt

2 cups flour
4 eggs - well beaten
cup sugar
2 teaspoon baking powder
1 lb. candied cherries
1 lb. candied pineapple
pecans

Bread & Butter Pickles
cups sliced cucumbers
6 onions sliced   Makes 8 pints.
Pour ⅓ cup salt over onions and cucumbers
and let stand for 3 hours. Rinse and drain.
Combine:
5 cups sugar
1½ tsp. Turmeric
1½ tsp. celery seed   2 TBSP mustard seed
over cucumber   3 cups vi...

35-40
immediately